PRACTICAL MANAGEMENT CONSULTING

Savio Gomes

First Step
Publishing
Paving Ways For New Writers

PRACTICAL MANAGEMENT CONSULTING

Savio Gomes

First Step Publishing
Paving Ways For New Writers

First Published in 2018 by First Step Publishing

Editorial / Sales / Marketing Office at
303-304 Garnet Nirmal Lifestyles Ph 2
Behind Nirmal Lifestyles Mall
LBS Marg Mulund West
Mumbai 400080
E-Mail:- info@firststepcorp.com
www.firststepcorp.com

ISBN:- 978-93-83306-46-6
Cover Designed by: Design Fishing
Price: INR 950 India and Rest USD 15

Dedicated to

My loving wife Mallika *[without whom this book would not have been possible]*
My father Peter Xavier Gomes

Inspired by [in no particular order]:

Stephen Ignatius Gomes	Mohan Mahajan
Keki Elavia	Sheetal Mane
Manoj Kabra	no longer with us
Patrick D'Souza	Gulati Satvinder Singh Pal
Nawshir Mirza	Milind Phadke
Kersi Fouzdar	no longer with us
Murzban Narsang	no longer with us
R Raghavan	no longer with us
Prof. Henry Desai	Prof. Mrs. Iyer

Based on experiences in various countries with P C Hansotia, Sea Green South Hotel, Moti Mahal Group of Restaurants, Sharp & Tannan, AF Ferguson, Crompton Greaves, Universal Ferro & Allied Chemicals, Mahajan & Aibara, Ernst & Young, KPMG, Kuwait Finance & Investment Company, Multi Trend International, Kout Food Group, KFGR UK, BDO and Al Homaizi Group.

Supported by the Patients Helping Foundation of Kuwait and the renal dialysis unit at Al Salaam Hospital, Dr Anas, Heidi & Rouffy. Dr Girish Warwadekar, Dr Ramakanta Panda, Dr Manimara Chozhan, Dr Zahir Hussain and others.

Table of Contents

1. Introduction 7
2. Definition 10
3. Components of Consulting [HFPSR] 16
4. Tools 18

   4.1   Sampling 19

   4.2   Networking 23

   4.3   Communication 25

   4.4   Benchmarking 29

   4.5   Cost Management 37

   4.6   Organization Structures 55

   4.7   Business Valuations 65

   4.8   Statistics 75

   4.9   Consulting Proposals 79

   4.10 Value Engineering 91

   4.11 Authority Matrix 97

   4.12 Succession Planning 102

   4.13 Profitability Improvement 105

   4.14 Process Reengineering 113

   4.15 Risk Management 121

   4.16 Policies and Procedures 130

   4.17 Business Plans 137

   4.18 Scenarios 148

4.19 Critical Path Method 153

4.20 Feasibility Studies 156

4.21 Intangibles 160

4.22 Internal Audit 165

4.23 Financial Reports and Audits 169

4.24 Analytical Review 173

4.25 Human Resources 178

4.26 Asset Allocation 187

4.27 Corporate Governance 191

4.28 Business Models 195

4.29 Transactions 205

4.30 Negotiations 215

4.31 Decision Making & DSS 229

4.32 Cash Flows 240

4.33 Employee Stock Options 247

4.34 LBOs & MBOs 253

4.35 Linear Programming [LP] 257

4.36 Quality Circles [QC] 263

4.37 Total Quality Management [TQM] 268

4.38 Six Sigma 273

4.39 Knowledge Management 278

4.40 Business Forecasts 285

1. Introduction

This book is written in an easy to understand style for budding management consultants. It can also serve as a hand book for management consultants whilst on projects. Executives working in various functions in private sector organizations, may also use this book to structure approaches or even solutions to challenges which they are confronted with. This is an excellent book for the aspiring [student] of management consulting in preparation for a career move. It encapsulates the career experiences of the author spanning 36 years of work experience. Management executives generally will find this book as a good discussion of possible approaches to various typical business challenges.

Management consulting is a career, not a job. A consultant must be technically sound, good at interpersonal relationships, excellent at communications and presentations, well networked and have high integrity & reliability. A consultant is constantly challenged to deliver exceptional value and design effective solutions. A consultant is judged, rewarded and satisfied by the implementation of solutions. A consultant is not always optimally successful and there are occasions when the client will feel disadvantaged. There are a number of constraints within the business environment which will challenge the consultant.

Within each section, the book includes several relevant examples to explain each aspect being discussed. What the book, therefore provides is examples of when different techniques or tools may be used by a management consultant.

The purpose of the book is to provide the basic understanding and tools required to be a successful consultant and achieve desired results, to improve or assist in improving organizational effectiveness. A consultant, or the consultant's team or in collaboration with the client team should deliver more value than the client team would on its own, and ideally more value than the client expects.

The book includes practical hints and tips that will aid in the practice of management consulting. The reader attempting application of some of these techniques is encouraged to refer other technical sources and examples to review alternative paths before applying these to a client situation. There are often numerous alternative solutions. Practice makes perfect and the more adventurous the consultant is, the better s/he gets at developing solutions for clients.

The book does not include detailed technical discussions of many approaches that are otherwise conveniently available on the internet or in well-known technical publications.

The author has over 30 years' of professional experience and works as a financial advisor. He has served as a financial accountant, internal auditor, advisory services professional and management consultant. The author has carried out projects in many cities in India and in several other countries (UK, Australia, USA, Kuwait, Saudi Arabia, Iraq, Iran, Bahrain, Dubai, Holland, Armenia, and Kenya). Difference in business environments, specific business circumstances, cultural differences, and trade practices account for different solutions to the same challenges.

2. Definition

What is Management Consulting? Why do we have management consulting at all? How does it differ from advisory services?

Consulting is active intervention, implementation, on-going monitoring and follow through. A management consultant constructs solutions [hopefully optimal] and implements them. Monitoring of results is an important function of a management consultant. A management consultant/ or Consulting therefore differs significantly from the Advisory services offered by Audit and Accountancy firms.

Example1: A consultant would devise a new process flow for Finance or HR or Production and assist with implementation and take a snap shot at three month intervals to ensure that the process flow is operating as intended and the desired benefits are in fact realized in a stable and sustainable manner. An advisory report would simply suggest alternative improved process flows or some fine tuning required to the existing process in line with 'leading' practices in the sector.

Example2: For a new business, a consultant c/ would provide a feasibility study together with monthly budgets, cash flows, organization chart, recruitment plan, assist with recruiting key management personnel, provide an information memorandum that can be used to raise funds, business plan and even participate in the fund raising process including the initial fund allocation.

An advisory service on the other hand would merely include the feasibility study with 5 year projections, estimated net present value and payback period. This advisory feasibility study would probably be used to be presented to funding agencies/ institutions. A Consultant would need to demonstrate a much deeper understanding of the issues affecting the business and the sector as compared with a generic, in principle advisory format feasibility study. The advisory feasibility study would be:

    (a) Subject to numerous limitations [e.g. market study not carried out]

    (b) Include a large number of disclaimers

    (c) Place responsibility on the management itself for all key assumptions and projections.

A consultant is concerned with results and the effectiveness of decisions and actions. A consultant is often compensated with reference to results.

Consulting aids in the definition of objectives and problems, and then researches and examines feasible solutions. In several situations, a consultant may be engaged to precisely, or better define the challenge. Quite often an organization is only broadly aware of a problem and the real core issues could very well lie elsewhere.

Example3: An organization ArtCo faces an issue of high employee turnover leading to inefficiencies, lower productivity and high recruitment costs. A consultant could be engaged to define ArtCo's problem more precisely, in terms of pay grades, skill sets, geographies, working conditions, reasons for separations, departments where incidence of separation is higher, roles and market conditions.

To consult in the business world is to intervene positively, to act in the interests of principal shareholders.

A consultant is necessarily multi skilled, professionally grounded in at least one technical discipline (engineering, human resources, financial etc.) with an all-round understanding of human resources, finance and project implementation.

The knowledge and understanding of operations research techniques, statistical techniques, economics, process analysis & improvement and financial analysis are useful consulting tools. Similarly, the understanding of human resources management, development of business strategies, plans, and tactical objectives are important pieces of the effective consulting process. A consultant also needs to have a fairly good understanding of both macroeconomics and microeconomics. How demand, supply and pricing may behave and interact, the impact of inflation, unemployment, rise/ fall in interest rates, rise/ fall in foreign exchange rates, government spending, taxation, demonetization, indirect taxes/ taxes on expenditure etc.

Advisory services are, in comparison, fairly limited scope. To advise is to put forth an informed view, perhaps based on past experiences or similar situations in other industries/ sectors. An advisor takes on a lower level of responsibility than a consultant. An advisor is not overly concerned with the ultimate results of management actions, and management is fully responsible for its choices and actions.

The advisor does not engage in selection of the optimum solution. Furthermore, the advisor rarely engages in the implementation of the solution. The consultant takes ownership for results. An advisor would present a range of alternative solutions with their pros and cons and different scenarios based on various assumptions. Management may choose to apply different assumptions or a different solution.

Example4: An advisor may develop a forecast or a budget [financial model] assuming a given rate of inflation, price increases and growth in market demand. The management may disagree and assume different values for each independent variable, based on its own intimate knowledge of the business in particular and the sector in general.

Value addition through the process of management consulting flows from the process of implementation, the process of actions, the process of follow up and follow through. Increased value addition is expected to be reflected in higher net revenues when properly presented to and perceived by customers.

A management consultant often derives a significant portion of her/ his fees from the results [value] delivered, based on successful implementation. An advisor delivers a report, a 'deliverable' and thus fulfills a contract leading to a billable service.

Example5: A tax consultant would research, review, construct a tax plan and the relevant deferred tax asset or liability schedules, put up a detailed plan for claiming tax benefits or deferring tax charges and then verify that such claims or corresponding returns have been filed with the relevant authorities within the stipulated time frames. A tax advisor would recommend alternative tax plans or tax structures for each jurisdiction with the relevant implications. Some professional bodies however, prohibit the payment of fees which are contingent upon results. For example the tax consultant may not charge his fees based on a scale of lower tax payments made by the client.

All of this is of course quite different from the classical jokes about management consultants sourcing information (and solutions) from clients and providing irrelevant information [sheep, time, balloons].

3. Components of Consulting [HFPSR]

What then are the main components of management consulting?

1. H: Analysis of the human dimension and dynamics of the situation and challenge from a people and organizational perspective
2. F: Financial analysis and evaluation
3. P: Process charting, work flow analysis, document flow, information flow analysis
4. S: Review of business strategy, goals, objectives and specific situational tactics
5. R: Resource review, resource management effectiveness review. This would include the review of human capital, information technology and funding. Economically speaking, resources are also factors of production.

There is no specific order of priority and the different components may assume varying degrees of importance in different situations, business and market environments.

It is an error of principle to start out each project in the very same manner. This (similar methodology

16

or product based solutions) is what generally reduces the effectiveness of consulting projects carried out by large firms. Firms that employ senior level experienced resources in client service delivery, and are flexible to adopt an objective situation driven approach as opposed to product – methodology driven approaches, are more likely to design and implement effective, efficient solutions.

Sadly, for the student, HFPSR is not a nice sounding, easy to remember acronym.

4. Tools

The tools in this chapter are not mentioned in order of importance. Consulting tools employed will depend upon:

  a. The nature of the project, which components are more important to a particular challenge and business environment. For example statistical or mathematical models are not always feasible.
  b. The speed with which results are required
  c. The dynamics of the operating environment.

The consultant is encouraged to build his tool box [also referred to as power pack] over time, retaining solutions, client cases, client operating metrics and a rich reference library.

It helps to cultivate the reading habit, broadens the horizons, learn new concepts. Subscribe to leading thought leadership publications. Remember what happened to the dinosaurs? Keep up to date and evolve. That you are reading this is very encouraging.

4.1   Sampling

A consultant needs an effective sample of what s/ he is studying. It is usually not possible to study all the individual items affected by the situation or the challenge. The sample should be reasonably random and should cover all types/ categories of items. For this purpose the consultant may stratify the items into groups to ensure that all groups are represented in the sample.

Example6: A study of contracts which may be subject to taxes should cover contracts for production, services, support services and operations, employment contracts, risk management contracts etc. Whilst all of the contracts need not be studied, a representative sample would give a fair idea of the tax implications.

Example7: A study of labour or exit interviews. The consultant may review a sample of exit interviews across departments, functions, divisions, pay grades, geographies, age groups, sex, and length of employment with the firm.

Samples for voluminous number of transactions may be generated using appropriate software and statistical sampling techniques. Very often a consultant may simply interview relevant personnel and select sample items at random after ensuring that all classes of items have been covered.

It is important for the consultant to review the sample with the client before the commencement of the study. This will help eliminate later discussions about bias in the sample, incompleteness of the sample or inappropriateness of the sample.

Example8: A sample of vendor account balances which either does not include small year end balances, accounts with few transactions, accounts with nil year end balances, or over emphasizes accounts with large balances/ a large number of transactions, could be later challenged on the grounds of sampling bias.

Sample sizes and items may have to be revised and reselected if after the study the results reveal bias or inappropriateness of the sample.

Example9: A sample of employees leaving may later reveal that almost all of the sampled instances related to a specific division, manager or geography. In this instance the consultant would need to increase the sample size and make an effort to select a more diverse sample from the total given population of employees leaving.

Example10: A sample of finished product from a new plant during trial production will reveal the strengths, weaknesses, physical and chemical properties of the finished product. For example, in pharmaceutical companies, food processing, cement [strength of bagged or ready mix for onsite use] and steel [sheets or coils] production.

Sampling reduces the effort of studying much more volumes of data. If properly constructed, the analysis of a sample may often, even provide better understanding than obtained by studying all the data items. It is often not possible in business situations to study all of the data items.

Example11: A company Super Pads produces industrial specification water proof pads. Units of production are rejected on a daily basis during quality control tests. The automated production line picks units at random for quality control tests such as stress tests and water proofing tests. The consultant may not be able to study, individually all of the thousands of units rejected each week by the automated production line.

As mentioned earlier, avoidance of bias in choosing sample units and choosing a representative sample are critical to effectively using sampling techniques.

Example12: In the above example, if the consultant only selects units rejected during a particular time of the day, or during a specific shift supervisor's duty time or batches produced with a particular grade/ supplier of material, then the conclusions drawn may not be feasible for the entire production process.

The concept of sampling is of course as old as Noah's ark. At the time, two of each species apparently sufficed.

4.2   Networking:

A key skill for successful consultants is networking. Networking helps of course in business development. However, networking also provides a consultant with critical sources of information, at times, anonymous. A consultant feeds off a multitude of information sources about industries, business performances, markets, products, sectors, innovation trends in processes, and hard data sources. Information is often not formally available or published, especially specific process related information.

Example13: Networking may provide the consultant with examples of industries or sectors that have usefully employed flexible labour hour practices. Networking may also provide consultants with information on how other retail lenders have reduced the time required to approve [or not] loan applications, respond to and address customer complaints, improve raw material yield percentages etc.

Example14: Networking may provide a consultant with useful information relating to estimates of sales growth, customer traffic, investments in new businesses/ expansion or bank deposits which are not otherwise published or available from regulatory authorities. For example although the statistical division of a central bank would have branch wise information on deposits and loans of commercial banks, it would hardly be expected to share this information with competing banks.

Networking is a critical skill and success factor, in some situations the most critical. Consultants cannot be isolated or operate in a vacuum. They need to be fully connected with the trends in their consulting universe. Building a network takes years of patience and develops through good inter personal relationships over a number of years, often going back to student days.

Example15: A tax consultant may through his network/ informal sources be informed about upcoming changes in tax legislation and rules which may impact the tax plans of his client. An elimination of a tax haven status, an upcoming double taxation treaty, an impending remittance/ withholding or capital gains tax, an upcoming environment/ sweet tax could have serious financial implications for a business enterprise.

If consultants were half as well networked as criminals, they would find solutions quicker.

4.3   Communication

A consultant must be very good at communication. Good communication is needed before, during and after designing a solution to ensure implementation. The level, mode and content of communication must take into account who the intended recipient is, in order to be effective.

Communication includes:
  (a) Listening carefully to what is said
  (b) Listening carefully to what is unsaid is often equally, if not more important
  (c) Speaking precisely
  (d) Rely on facts more than opinions
  (e) Not speaking when silence is the better option
  (f) Clear, precise well written communications including e mails
  (g) Expert, professional use of presentation software tools. Nothing amuses/ upsets clients more than amateurish MS PowerPoint templates
  (h) Good stand up presentation skills. Nothing is more irksome than a consultant who reads from a presentation and/ or has his back turned to the audience while facing the screen/ or has his hands placed in his pockets

(i) Professional sense of dress. A consultant who wears a dark suit with a pink tie and brown shoes will cut a poor impression likewise a consultant who troops in for a meeting straight out of bed having plastered his hair with gel

(j) Good etiquette at a meeting. Knowing when to sit, when to stand, when to stop speaking, where to sit (occupying the head seat at the table is not likely to score points with the client), not tapping the table or swiveling around in the chair, not liberally partaking of refreshments during a meeting, making inconvenient or inappropriate demands for refreshments

(k) When and how to hand out your business card. Do not make an exaggerated show of humility while handing out your business card. That works in Japan [along with a deep bow], anywhere else it looks silly. A business card is simply a means of establishing a communication link

(l) Not raising one's voice at meeting held to discuss a situation. If you raise your voice in excitement, the content of the message will get distorted. The other person may also respond in a raised tone and from then on, the meeting goes rapidly downhill.

Likewise do not respond in a raised tone if the other person does so

(m) Not getting emotionally attached to ideas or principles. Let logic and facts prevail. If you concede when you are not quite right, you will earn respect

(n) Always be on time, preferably a few minutes early for a meeting to allow for contingencies and settling in or set up time. Being late is not fashionable [any longer?]

(o) Always carry an adequate supply of visiting cards readily available and appropriate writing materials. Rummaging around before or during or after a meeting is clumsy

(p) Communicate promptly. Undue delays without holding responses explaining the reasons for the delay create a poor impression. It is always good practice to reply promptly, even if it is only to acknowledge and is only a holding reply.

Everything that a consultant says or does or does not, contribute toward the clients' perception of the consultant. An aggregation of this through multiple incidents, and a consultant develops a reputation.

A good politician is a good communicator. A politician is only as good as his spin doctor.

4.4 Benchmarking

Benchmarking includes comparing:
  (a) Practices
  (b) Processes, and
  (c) Financial results.

A consultant may carry out benchmarking formally, by reaching out to other organizations. They may contribute information and even to the costs of the benchmarking study. The results of the benchmarking are usually shared to all those who contributed, while keeping the specific identities anonymous. The benchmarking report would report data for Companies A, B, C etc. in no particular order to retain anonymity.

Example16: Benchmarking of salary levels across competitors by a firm wanting to understand if its salary levels are competitive enough and will attract the best talent available.

Example17: Benchmarking of key performance indicators for chief financial officers or chief operating officers. The ownership is trying to set right the expectations from the role of CFO/ COO and the balance between the role, responsibility, accountability and compensation. One way of doing this is to look at how some other business firms measure and reward performance for these roles.

Example18: Benchmarking of sales incentives or bonus plans. A company may need to incentivize its sales teams to deliver higher sales growth, especially if there is a good flow through to the bottom line and higher sales inevitably leads to higher profits. Different companies in the industry could have a mix of short term, long term, cash and non-cash incentives, share options or even deferred payment benefits. Incentive plans could be designed with the objective of attracting or the objective of retaining key human resources.

Example19: Benchmarking of production wastage and yields in the steel or cable industry. Integrated steel plants producing hot roll coils or steel profiles of standard industry size can compare input output ratios, energy consumption, wastage and rejections. Cutting off the ends of sections can lead to considerable wastage [only some of which is recycled]. Similarly, producers of jelly filled cables or optical fibre cables, experience varying degrees of production wastage and rejected lengths particularly, for relatively newer units where production processes have not been stabilized as yet.

The consultant engaging in benchmarking must as far as possible is aware of differences between firms in:

(a) Policies and practices
(b) Processes [e.g. the extent of automation, the type of equipment used]
(c) Organization structure, and
(d) Organization life cycle

The purpose of benchmarking is for a firm to identify leading practices, better practices and improve processes and financial results. Implementation however, is not recommended unless the reasons for the differences in reported results are carefully studied and fully understood.

The consultant may be able to explain some key differences in financial results and processes as a result of differences in the strategy, policies and life cycles of the firms.

Example20: A firm with a more mature established brand or product may have a different policy toward hiring, retaining and incentivizing senior management roles, as compared with a new entrant firm aiming to grow at a very rapid pace and catch up with the industry leaders. A firm with a large production capacity may be able to purchase inputs at a lower cost due to the much larger quantity required. A firm closer to the markets will incur a lower distribution cost as compared with a producer set up closer to the source of raw material. A new entrant firm may be set up in a State which provides concessional power, concessional land, tax free holidays and housing subsidies for employees. A firm with a high degree of process automation could have better input output ratios, fewer rejections and quicker production times with better planning. However, the return on assets for such a firm could be lower because of the larger investment required up front in the automated processes.

Results of benchmarking can be presented through tables, diagrams, charts or process flow charts. The objective is to visually present the results in a manner that facilitates meaningful comparison and interpretation leading to goal setting. In manufacturing concerns, visual displays of benchmark data and targets are often set up at shop floor and/ or in marketing departments, as a reminder of where the firm is in the market place.

At the operational level, benchmarking can be used to set stretch targets. If the objective is to beat the competitions, benchmarks can be used to encourage the teams to gain a step over competition,

Example21: A mobile telephone company may benchmark out the number of prepaid and postpaid lines which the various competitive firms have in the same market. A company installing elevators may benchmark the number of new units installed in the same market versus competitors and the number of new buildings or the growth in the real estate sector. An ERP solution firm could benchmark versus the number of potential client companies in the market installing other ERP solutions and its own clients.

Example22: Shop floor wastage in an industrial products firm, or wastage in a food production unit or a restaurant chain. A firm, TEDP producing machine tools for the automobile industry incurs a certain amount of shop floor wastage and also consumption of materials 'consumables' during the production process for given volumes. A food production unit of say, croissants, sandwiches, cakes, tarts or pastry will incur a certain amount of production wastage of materials. In addition, gaps in sales and production planning will result in date expiry issues with product either having to be destroyed or sold at low prices near date expiry or donated. It is possible to benchmark such factors.

A retail lending firm can benchmark the incidence of delays and/ or defaults.

Example23: Benchmarking of amount spent on marketing by dot com B2B or B2C firms versus new customers gained or eyeballs gained. Some firms spend huge sums on gaining new customers, and these impacts profitability even though sales increases. A firm which delivers consumer goods to the door by accepting on line sales orders incurs various costs such as marketing, incorrect deliveries, customer rejections etc. Industry or market standards are usually available which can be used for benchmarking. Funding agencies such as private equity firms usually have established benchmarks for such business process results.

Example24: Amounts spent on marketing a particular product versus sales revenue [daily newspapers, personal care products, baby food, potato chips, chocolate, home furnishings, air conditioners, airline tickets]. A sports team [cycling, baseball, basketball, cricket, soccer] may incur huge costs of securing premium sportspersons, whereas sponsorship and advertising revenue streams at some point may fall short, if results do not materialize as expected.

For best results, the stretch targets based on benchmarking, are then visually displayed at the production site [shop floor or central kitchens] and monitored versus actuals on a frequent basis, even hourly/ daily/ weekly/ monthly. To be meaningful, the stretch targets should take into account operational and process differences between the firms being compared.

There is little point in making comparisons if one team or firm clearly has superior equipment, access to more funding, better facilities and infrastructure generally, better coaches/ personnel and a longer history of perfecting their practices.

Example25: There is little point in comparing an Indian/ Russian or Chinese car manufacturer with GM/ Ford/ Chevrolet/ Toyota. There is little point in comparing a Chinese passenger jet with an Airbus or Boeing, where the differences in the research and development experience are simply staggering. In general, the more complex and nonstandard the business processes are, the more difficult it is to usefully employ benchmarking.

Example26: A country may like to benchmark taxation rates [direct or indirect] or central bank base lending rate or the cost of holding a sporting event [Asian Games, Olympics, Winter Olympics etc.] or costs of providing power, or per capita carbon emission. There are huge differences in the business, social and cultural environments, which would result in very limited utility of such comparisons and the impact of any such event or decision.

Everybody compares all the time. That is human nature, comparison leads to envy, and envy is bottomless. The principle behind benchmarking is to make meaningful, logical and useful comparisons.

4.5   Cost Management

The success of a business depends equally on the growth of revenues [sales] and the management of costs. The understanding of the nature of various costs in each situation, is therefore essential to a consultant.

Direct costs increase directly in proportion to sales. Direct costs could be fuel, input materials or labour directly engaged on production.

Example27: Cost of food, cost of steel or copper, cost of iron ore in a steel plant, cost of limestone or energy in a cement plant, cost of energy in a furnace operation, cost of coffee in a coffee shop, cost of potato in a potato chip plant.

Example28: A factory Steelcrej produces a wide range of storage units [cupboards and shelves] with locks, open, with glass/ without, with wood/ steel features, with safe boxes and without and a wide range of safe boxes/ lockers.   The factory is not profit making. A consultant is engaged to review which products are not profitable. A detailed review of both direct and indirect costs such as marketing would reveal which products are more profitable at the gross margin level [after direct costs] and which products are profitable at the net profit level after depreciation, marketing costs and other overheads including design & development costs. It may be that high volume sales products have actually lower gross margins [sales minus direct costs] and that products with low sales actually have the highest gross margins. Management, based on the results of the consultant's analysis may decide to discontinue certain products/ lower the prices of some products or increase the prices of other products or bundle some products and their pricing together. For example the prices of a safe box or a locker may be reduced if it is ordered by a customer together with a storage system.

Overhead costs or Overheads are costs that are shared across production units. Overheads do not directly add value to the product or service. Overheads function as business support elements. The general objective of every business firm is to keep overhead costs to a minimum. Overhead costs increase the risks of the business since these costs are incurred irrespective of the level of business activity.

Example29: Consulting firm A opens offices in several countries. The overheads incurred are office rents, office administration staff, minimum number of consulting personnel office overhead such as transportation, utilities, printing, hardware etc. The volume of consulting business in some countries falls sharply due to geopolitical reasons. The overhead will continue to be incurred until the firm is able to exit the market. Consulting firm B does not establish offices but flies in personnel when needed for projects. The costs of Consulting firm B are direct costs and vary with the level of projects.

Example30: Costs of common central functions such as corporate office, human resources, finance, information technology, compliance, risk management, and quality control. As businesses grow [profitably], there is a tendency to take eyes off central overhead which can soon mushroom into a burden. Especially in low margin businesses, central costs are a luxury and should be minimized. A low cost entry level automobile manufacturer will spend less on marketing and distributor displays than a premium, full options high end technology automobile manufacturer. Costs of information technology systems can often be huge, in terms of onetime installation/ implementation costs as well as ongoing maintenance, updates and annual license fees. The benefits of acquiring such systems and installing such overhead must be carefully compared with the potential benefits. The benefits are at best potential and yet to be realized, whereas, the cash outflow on the costs are certainties.

Example31: A retail company Maclin, selling boxes of stationery or medical equipment, works out each additional overhead item in terms of additional sales units needed. For example a conference for management in another country would be covered by X000 units of additional sales. This helps to maintain focus on profitability. The number of sales units is the internal currency of the company. A training program or a marketing program proposed could cost $ XXX or $X0,000 equivalent units of additional sales to cover this item of overhead, given that the company knows the profitability per unit sold.

Overheads can be variable or fixed [or semi variable/ fixed]. Overheads that are fixed do not increase in proportion to activity levels [production or sales]. However, they increase the firm's risk levels since they also do not reduce when the activity level is reduced.

Example32: A firm's costs to sustain a corporate office with a central financial reporting function will rarely decrease by ten percent when sales fall by ten percent. A consulting/ legal firm's costs of maintaining an internal library or database will not increase or decrease with the change in the number of clients or revenue earned. A manufacturing plan at a remote location sets up company guest houses to accommodate company personnel and business visitors. These costs will not reduce if production is higher or lower within a given range of activity. The capital costs and maintenance costs are already committed.

Example33: A firm's internal library and product innovation research facility, or a stud farm has a minimum amount of equipment for exercising/ treating stallions, colts and fillies. The cost of maintaining a racecourse is committed irrespective of the number of races held.

Example34: Warehouse and storage costs are largely fixed as a fixed amount of space is rented or constructed for dry, cold and chilled storage. These costs do not vary if volumes rise or fall unless additional space is needed. If however, the warehouse is outsourced, some contractual arrangements could include clauses that vary costs with the amount of product actually stored.

Total costs are the total costs including both direct and indirect to deliver a product or service. Total costs are rarely relevant to make decisions such as make or buy, increase/ decrease in production volumes, outsource or in house, pricing etc. unless specific funding constraints are involved.

Sunk costs are costs that are already invested [sunk]. These costs are very difficult, if not impossible to change, except on major restructuring or exit of the business.

Example35: A constructed shop floor, a dentist's chair, a path-laboratory equipment a decorated restaurant, a helipad on a building, or a corporate office are examples of sunk costs. A minimum amount of mining equipment and overburden earth moving vehicles are sunk costs in a mining operation. Similarly, in a chemical plant, a blender or packaging unit is a sunk cost for a given capacity. Those costs have been incurred even if the capacity is only partially utilized. A retail product distribution company may have paid a territory fee to acquire rights to trade in a particular territory. The territory fee is a sunk cost, the royalty/ franchise fee linked to sales is a direct cost.

Example36: The land purchased for a production unit is a sunk cost. It is often not fully utilized even after space for the production unit itself, administration buildings and storage space for raw materials and finished product. Any incremental revenue from this sunk costs will help. For example, a rental for a telecommunication tower or a transmission line on the land would bring in revenue without additional costs.

Total costs and sunk costs are usually generally irrelevant for business decisions. The capital amounts have already been committed and future business decisions will not change these amounts.

Example37: Amounts already spent on a shop floor on an extruder or a paint shop are not relevant to deciding whether to take on production of a new product if spare capacity [machine hours] is already available. The shop floor itself may be large enough to accommodate an additional production line. The classic example of a sunk cost is of course a swimming pool.

Marginal costs are the amount by which costs increase by producing one additional unit.

Marginal utility in economic terms is the additional amount of satisfaction for a consumer by consuming one additional unit. The principle is the same. Marginal utility however, decreases with increases in volumes, whereas marginal costs are mostly variable and often do not decrease substantially with increases in volume.

Example38: In an audit or consulting firm, marginal salary costs may actually be nil, if the work for new client can be supported by the existing team [which is why services can have a large profit margin] and overtime is not paid to professional staff.

Example39: In a mining company, the amount by which additional explosives or equipment or labour hours are needed to produce additional tons of ore, are marginal costs. In farming operation, additional seed, fertilizers and pesticides are marginal costs.

Example40: In a retail finance company, the number of additional marketing representatives needed to penetrate a new segment [e.g. office workers in a particular district] or a new territory, to generate additional customers or additional loan amounts granted.

Example41: A team of accountants at CATec which performs outsourced accounting services for small businesses may use the same information technology assets and staff to take on additional clients [up to a point]. Marginal costs are, therefore, virtually nil to take on a new client and the team can quote a lower [competitive] fee to gain new business. The CATec team say, is set up to take on board 10 clients. The team has 7 clients. The additional 3 clients may not cost the team any additional resources as there is spare capacity. A shop floor has the capacity to produce 1,000 units per day of a machined component. It currently has orders for around 600 units per day. The firm may quote competitively lower to gain orders of another 400 units per day since the marginal costs are minimum, virtually only the direct material costs, since the labour and machine costs are already committed. Of course the assumption being that customers do not complain about the differential pricing.

Costs behave differently over time. A cost which is variable may turn out to be more fixed in nature in the long run and vice versa.

Example42: An expanding business, after a point may need more space for offices and shop floor or more production/ storage areas. The warehouse space even though outsourced may not be adequate for higher business volumes. A dentist with more patients may need to add dentist chairs. A car servicing or wash station may need additional lines as business volumes grow. A hospital may need additional beds or operation theatres over time. A yarn manufacturing unit may need additional machines, additional dyeing equipment as volumes of sales grow. An outsourcing information technology firm may need to add servers for various operations including back up once client business volumes exceed a threshold.

Sometimes, for ease of accounting, firms account for costs on projects on the basis of standards [standard costs]. Therefore, based on expectations, a firm may set up a standard cost per hour of labour/ management time or a standard cost per machine hour. If standards are reasonably accurate, they can save the time involved in quickly accounting for actual costs.

Example43: A firm which uses iron sheets may purchase them during the year at various price from various vendors. The firm may set up a standard purchase or input cost of $ XX per ton to simplify the cost workings on different jobs and quote competitive selling prices. A pharmaceutical company may purchase bulk drugs used in formulations from various supply points. For purposes of accounting, inventory valuation and pricing a standard cost is used in the system. Variances between standards and actual total costs of the input are eliminated periodically, with the difference apportioned to inventory [raw, work in progress and finished] and the income statement for the period [for goods sold]. A firm producing chocolate may purchase sugar, chocolate and butter at different times of the year, at different prices and from different sources [variations in duties, taxes and forwarding costs]. For purposes of pricing the finished product, the firm may prefer the use of standard costs for all batches, the standard cost approximating the average purchase cost for a year.

The use of standard costs is often times more practical and convenient than using a moving weighted average of actual costs. The moving weighted average of costs would keep changing with each transaction and, therefore a stable basis for pricing and management decisions would not be available. Activity results would also not be comparable across different time periods. Standard costs are convenient to use when raw materials are procured from a number of sources at different times of the year, at different prices.

Standard costs should be reviewed and reassessed for closeness to actuals on an annual basis. Standards which are too far from actuals and result in large year end variances, have very limited usefulness in understanding the results of operations [say, quarterly] or in pricing and other business decisions.

Why is cost measurement and management important. A consultant seeking to improve profitability will target the major cost heads, in addition to looking at ways to increase revenues. Most profitability exercises begin with costs reductions which may be possible without compromising the quality of products or services to customers.

A cost increased, is simply cash out of the door and does not return once expended. Costs increased not only decrease profitability, but may significantly decrease the valuation of a business.

Example44: A firm incurs additional costs toward sponsorship of a sports event, however, sales do not increase substantially and the profit for the year falls by $ 500,000. Since the business is valued at a multiple of 6x the earnings, the valuation of the business [relevant to investors and bankers] in fact falls by $ 3million which operational head usually do not appreciate. A firm adds quality control personnel and additional grades of managers at the production unit. The annual salary bill for the company increases by $ 1mn, the value of the business may be eroded to the extent of $ 6mn, if compensating improvements in profitability do not occur. A firm increases the fixed monthly salaries of employees instead of paying out an incentive or bonus. The operation heads feel that as compared with paying out a $10mn bonus, they have saved the company money by agreeing to a $7mn salary increase. However, the salary increase is a permanent increase which cannot be reduced in times of reduced sales. The firm's valuation is reduced by a market multiple of the $7mn. A firm incurs maintenance expenditure of over $5mn on machinery instead of purchasing new machinery. The $5mn is a recurring, annual cash expense and the firm's valuation is decreased by a market multiple, say 6x of $5mn or $30 mn.

Example45: Burspur, a cement plant will need to carefully review the input output ratios of various ores being used. Different batches may produce different grades of cement with different strengths or erosion characteristics. The price realized of each batch may depend upon the test results. The cost of the materials in a batch may be lower, however, the realized net selling prices could also be lower. It may be more efficient to use higher grade inputs.

Cost measurement and cost control of course helps to improve profitability. Money saved is money earned.

Example46: A company packs cement in paper bags, synthetic polythene bags and jute bags. Similarly with a company using paperboard or polystyrene boxes to deliver pizza. The cost of each of the bags/ boxes differs. In each case, the bursting strength of the bags may be retained although the thickness, fibre density may be marginally reduced, thus reducing costs of packing per unit. As with increases in costs, a reduction in costs which is sustainable can result in the valuation of the business increasing by a multiple of the savings generated. An airline finds a lower cost way of accepting/ generating bookings through an app or other online platform. The saving in costs generates a multiple of increase in company valuation.

However, in most business enterprises, the proper and accurate measurement of costs enables rational pricing of end products.

Example47: A proper understanding of costs would enable a publisher/ printer of books to price books based on the quality of paper used, the size of the book, the margins, colour features, effort required to design and edit etc. A proper understanding of costs of maintaining a prize racehorse or a bull, would enable proper pricing of the stud fee.

Example48: A poor understanding of costs could lead to lower than required pricing and operational losses. A small business firm Quik Jack accepts orders online and delivers printed t-shirts and cups as souvenirs or gift items. Quik Jack does not factor in the cost of delays in receiving payment from customers, the costs of holding inventory, the full cost of distribution, the costs of changes in the designs, costs of storage, the costs of product defects/ rejections. Quik Jack prices the product using only direct costs of material and labour. The product is under-priced and Quik Jack incurs a loss even though sales volumes have been good. An individual Sree, purchases books or mobile phones from a web platform during bargain months and commits prices to customers in his locality. He has not factored in the costs of distribution and product insurance or installation and/ or replacements in case of defects. Sree incurs a loss despite good sales volumes and a good gross margin.

Example49: An understanding of how costs are incurred over time and class, would enable an airline or a railway company to better align prices according to sectors/ timings/ seasons/ competition/ carryon baggage and other facilities such as lounge access and insurance. It is not uncommon for railways to charge differential fares during different day parts or for airlines to charge different prices over some routes and for some classes without frills. In some instances, the airline may be able to charge very low prices to cargo being shipped since there may be minimal marginal costs and the spare capacity [cargo space] is available on those routes.

This is the basic principle behind activity based costing [ABC]. ABC allows better cost allocation to production or service units in accordance with how costs are actually incurred. This allows differential pricing for different product features or services.

Example50: A textile company Raytex, may determine that the packing, distribution and marketing costs of its products differs very significantly for sales through its various sales channels such as, distributors, own retail shops, and the non-branded wholesale segment. A better understanding of these costs as incurred [the financial accounting system would simply aggregate all of these costs under the head 'packing' or 'distribution'] would enable better understanding of the pricing of these products can be varied across product units. A few cents [$] reduction or increase per unit could result in large increase in sales and profitability.

Example51: A cola distribution company may understand that smaller cans or bottles are far more expensive to produce than larger sized units and therefore, the larger units may be priced lower and not directly proportional to the liquid volume. A 1,000 ml can or bottle may be priced 12 times lower than a 100ml can or bottle instead of simply ten times lower. Similarly, a beverage of the same volume, but requiring chilled storage and distribution would cost more to distribute, store and sell.

Proper pricing could make the difference between gaining/ retaining and losing customers. Very often an entrepreneur who does not fully understand his business costs could make a loss by quoting a low price or lose customers by quoting a high price.

Example52: A consultant submitting a proposal for a restructuring project may under or overestimate the effort and resources required, and therefore may under or over price his proposal. A logistics firm or a construction firm submitting a quote/ tender may inaccurately under quote based on an incomplete understanding of the costs. The firm could incur a huge loss on the contract. A transport company may have fully utilized capacity, however, may have under-priced seats/ berths. The company would make a loss. If the company over prices the seats/ berths it would lose to competitors. A restaurant may under-price items on the menu, not taking into account establishment costs and add-ons. Even high sales may not result in a profit. A large food production company FPC produced croissants and tarts for a chain of coffee shops. The tarts were correctly priced and sold in smaller volumes. The croissants were under-priced and sold in large volumes, incurring a loss for the period during which FPC had committed to supply agreed quantities of the product. A student undertakes to distribute study notes and student questions to others. He factors in the cost of photocopying but does not fully take into the cost of distribution and the risk of non-payment. He is seriously out of pocket by the end of term.

Lack of proper understanding of costs can lead to disasters. Key wars and battles have been lost because of the failure to properly estimate the costs of invading Russia.

4.6   Organization Structures

Business firms, charitable or non-profit organizations can have a large variety of organization structures. Organization structures should be tailored according to the vision and mission of the organization. Consultants are often engaged to design or alter organization structures. As organizations grow, they often need either tweaks or dramatic changes to the organization structure.

The structure should be determined by the strategy [longer term] and the goals or tactics [shorter term] of the organization. The structure should help the organization achieve its objectives and goals.

Key aspects of determining an appropriate organization structure are:

(a) Key areas of responsibility and accountability
(b) Key performance indicators for the organization and individual roles
(c) Authority/ approval chain
(d) Specific job descriptions

An organization may adopt different types of structures, namely:

(a) A linear hierarchical reporting structure. Most business firms follow a linear structure, this however, does not mean that it is always the best structure. Armed forces follow a linear structure
(b) A project based structure. An oil exploration company for example or a real estate company could have a project based structure with different teams responsible for different aspects of the project, each construction site or exploration site would have a project team
(c) A flat structure with a number of equally responsible managers. Smaller firms and initial stage firms typically have a flat structure with a fewer number of employees and managers. Flat structures usually facilitate speedy

decision making since the chain of command is short. An investment company, a private equity company may have a flat structure to facilitate speedy decisions. Flat structures have fewer layers of management as compared with linear structures. A typical flat structure may have only three layers of management levels.

(d) A matrix structure with experienced professionals interacting with each other as needed to deliver a common goal.

Organizations may use a combination of such structures. An organization may use a typical linear structure, a project team for a new market entry or a project, and a matrix structure for a project involving various functions.

Example53: Company KGG produces automobile accessories and has a linear, function based organization structure. KGG wants to enter into a new market/ territory e.g. DRC, and KGG may form a project team to establish an office, marketing and compliance teams. DRC imposes a value added tax [VAT] and this impacts purchases, marketing, finance, information technology, and commercial departments. KGG develops a team with a matrix structure to implement VAT within a given time line, involving team members from various departments who will feed in to the information technology department the system changes needed.

Example54: An operations team at a factory [bulk drugs, engineering, manufacturing generally] would prefer an hierarchical structure, so do most military organizations based on a chain of command, core operations and support services. This enables focus on functions and specialization. The drawback is that each function sometimes acts as an independent silo and there are barriers to effective communication. Some linear/ hierarchical structures tend to have too many departmental and inter departmental meetings, leading to delays in decision making.

Example55: A consulting team would most likely use a project based structure where professionals of different discipline work together to deliver a common goal. A consulting team may employ a project consisting of a finance expert, a cost accountant, an engineer and an information technology consultant/s to carry out a project involving measurement and reporting of production costs on a timely basis.

Example56: A team of mathematicians working on solving a common problem would use a matrix structure. A company implementing a software platform such as an ERP would use a matrix structure. A matrix structure usually involves professional experts of different disciplines who need to collaborate on a project and share knowledge. Matrix structures are often used by product research, development and medical research teams.

The organization structure should be designed to deliver the goals of the company.

A common mistake is to design an organization structure around individual preferences, individual strengths and weaknesses of key management members. There are some organizations which have combined roles into individual positions, simply because a long standing employee has been deemed capable of those roles.

Example57: A company FKL faced a crisis of senior management. FKL had employed a senior internal auditor Selvy, reporting to the chairman for over 10 years. Selvy was given charge commercial, legal, purchasing and finance departments in addition to the internal audit role. Needless to say, the combination of roles created a conflict of interest and suboptimal functions leading to inefficiencies.

Example58: The legal and human resource function may report into the head of operations in a situation where the head of operations happens to have a legal background. A customer complaint recording and resolution function may be asked to report to the head of operations. Clearly these are sub optimal choices and will not deliver results desired or expected from these functions. In the case of FKL above, their problems were compounded by having the human resource function report to the head of operations [a trusted old hand] who was also in charge of recording and addressing customer complaints.

For purposes of independence and internal control certain functions should not logically report into each other. Internal controls are systems and procedures whereby the work of one person is independently verified by another as part of routine processes.

Example59: Finance/ internal audit / risk management. It is clearly not a good practice to have the internal audit function report to the chief financial officer or to the head of operations. Similarly, the risk manager should be independent and not report to the CFO or COO.

Example 60: Payroll processing and human resources. Payroll processing is usually better off reporting to Financial Control. If payroll processing is with Human Resources which also issues appointment letters and increment letters, there is a huge risk of inappropriate decisions. Similarly, Human resources and Production/ Operations should be set apart. If Human resources reports to Operations, there would be a lack of independence in matters of recruitment, exits, exit interviews, increments and promotions. Quality control and production operations should also be set apart. It is important that quality control has independence of carrying out checks and reporting the results of those checks.

Example61: Emission tests versus norms and crash tests for an automobile manufacturer should be carried out by persons/ teams independent of the production operation or product design teams. Automobile companies have been known to tamper with emission test results since the persons responsible were either the design or production teams.

However, in family managed firms where the persons responsible are stakeholders, this coupling of functions is common with family members supported by professionals who may be experts in different fields.

Example62: In a family owned conglomerate, one family member could be responsible for investor relations, releases to the stock exchange, raising of finance from financial institutions and acquisitions or disposals. Another family member/s may be solely responsible for oversight of operational profitability and maximizing return on assets and return on equity. In a multi brand company, one family member may be responsible for relationships with all the OEMs [original equipment manufacturers] or franchisors and for acquisition of new brand/ trade mark/ territory rights.

Example63: In a media software company producing programs, one family member could be responsible for production or selection of programs, and for marketing and another family member could be responsible for financing and planning returns distributed to shareholders, share buyback, holding or trading in treasury shares, raising additional capital at a premium. A third family member could be responsible for marketing in international territories.

The organization structure should be tailored to the specific needs of the firm:

(a) One firm may need an in-house legal manager or general counsel whereas another may be satisfied by using various external legal firms on a retainer or project basis

(b) A firm may need a CRO [chief reconstruction officer or chief reengineering officer] to coordinate all projects of that nature

(c) One firm may need a chief financial officer, whereas others may need a financial controller/ chief accountant/ finance manager/ chief internal auditor/ senior project accountant [where multiple expansion projects are in progress] or a senior management accountant. Each of these have different roles and responsibilities.

(d) A firm may need a warehouse manager and a purchasing manager. A larger firm may need a supply chain director who is responsible overall for purchasing, commercial, distribution and warehousing functions

Combining functions always carries the risk of dilution of internal financial or operational controls. However, in some organizations the size of the firm simply does not support different, independent functional heads.

Example64: A copper mine CMAT, in Australia has a Commercial Manager. The Commercial Manager oversees accounting, purchase, circulating and opening tenders [and responses], payments to suppliers and reconciliation of year end supplier's balances.

All religious foundations and criminal organizations too, have organization structures and authority-responsibility charts, only often not publicly visible.

4.7 Business Valuations

The valuation of businesses is both an art and a science. The consultant should be aware [and should accordingly limit or mark his report as such] of who the intended recipient is. The report could be for bankers/ financial institutions/ third party investors/ internal discussions by management for restructuring etc. There are several commonly used methodologies to establish a baseline value of a business:

(a) Multiple of cash flows
(b) Multiple of sales
(c) Net adjusted asset value
(d) Discounted cash flow
(e) Dividend earning capacity
(f) Multiple of net profits

Multiple of cash flows involve applying a multiple to the sustainable cash flows of a business. A careful understanding of the business, its sustainable operational results, cash required for servicing debt, cash required for capital expenditure, cash required for working capital, and taxes is required. Often in the context of a transaction this is determined independently through a due diligence process. A due diligence process may be undertaken by external independent advisors. Such advisors may be accountancy/ audit firms and/ or an independent advisor with expert knowledge of the relevant industry [e.g. telecom, steel, automotive].

The cash flows used may be for the latest available 12 month period, or for the immediately next 12 month period. For purposes of valuation a projection of cash flows may also be used. The degree of certainty attached to the cash flows decreases with the extension of the period over which cash flows are estimated.

Using a projection of cash flows has several drawbacks. Firstly, the projections are subject to numerous hypothetical assumptions, several of which may not hold good over time. Secondly, the multiple to be applied is largely guesswork as there is no way the multiple can be accurately estimated at the end of say, 5 years. And, finally, cash received after n number of years is not quite the same value as cash received in year 0 or year 1. This can to an extent be compensated for, by applying a discount rate. The discount rate must allow for an interest free rate, a risk premium and the time value of money. The risk premium could be specific to the business or to the industry, country etc.

The multiple applied is the multiples observed in recent transactions. Called the 'market multiple'. This should be multiples relevant to the specific industry, size of firm and size of transaction. Such information on multiples is usually publicly available or otherwise available with accountancy/ audit firms engaged in transaction advisory services. Multiples for larger transactions or multiples in specific countries may differ significantly from the average.

Market multiples are also applied to the sales number. In some industries the best way to value a firm is to examine the sales, and the quality [recurring, cash, credit etc.] of sales. Sales may be cash sales or sales for credit. The amount of sales sitting in receivables should be examined. Market multiple to sales is usually applied when the majority of sales are cash sales [e.g. gas stations, coffee shops, book stores] and the margins are well established. Sales multiples are best used also when sales are recurring and the frequency of such sales can be estimated with a high degree of certainty.

Example65: A sales revenue multiple can be used for a cinema theatre, allowing for seasonal fluctuations. Takings during holiday seasons may be much more. Sales multiples may also be applied to car rental revenues, sales revenue of a photograph studio, sales revenue of an event management company, sales revenue of a bookseller selling books to college students, sales of a city transport bus operator with well defined routes.

Net adjusted value establishes a baseline value for the business. This is the minimum value of the business. This method simply arrives at the net value of tangible assets which may be realized in a liquidation scenario. Usually the starting point is the latest available balance sheet. Adjustments [deductions] are made for costs of disposal, realizable values instead of carrying values and settlement values of liabilities instead of recorded liabilities. Realizable values are particularly used when the assets are relatively older, and are already heavily depreciated.

Example66: The value of inventory is reduced for non-saleable inventory values, either whole items or discounted inventory values for non-moving inventory. Fixed assets which are 'redundant' or not employed in the business in the production of revenue are excluded. For example a company may hold land which is not required for the purpose of the business. Liabilities may not have been fully recorded and these are deducted. Contingent liabilities may need to be taken into consideration, especially pending lawsuits, if the outcome at the date of valuation is likely to be adverse [may not have been adverse at the time of finalization of the financial statements]. On the other hand, some liabilities may be settled at less than their recorded values. A creditor or a lender may accept a lower amount in full settlement of a long outstanding debt paid in cash. An employee claiming long outstanding dues may prefer a smaller settlement instead of lengthy court proceedings, although the larger claim account may have been fully provided for in the financial statements.

Discounted cash flows [DCF] is a complex methodology of largely academic interest to buyers, and most often ignored in the real world between businessmen. This involves projecting the net cash inflows over future periods, and estimating the value of the business at the end of the period of projections. The assumptions about cash flows are subject to numerous explicit and implicit assumptions. The discount rate applied can vary depending upon the risk premium applied, the degree of certainty attached to the cash flows, market conditions etc. In the case of listed equities, the discount rate also depends upon the extent to which the movement in the stock price follows the stock prices of similar companies or a similar index. DCF places a high value typically on firms showing strong growth prospects but with little asset backing. Of all the methods, DCF usually results in the highest possible value of the firm.

DCF also involves estimating a terminal value. The terminal value is based on the rate of growth to perpetuity and the discount rate. The formula usually gives a very high terminal value. Often, while using DCF, consultants will instead simply estimate the terminal value at a multiple of the last year's cash profits, based on market trends or practices.

Example67: A tour firm, Melshak, which organizes desert or mountain or historical tours may not be asset heavy and may therefore usefully valued using DCF after allowing for operating costs, and applying a suitable discount rate. The terminal value of Melshak, may be estimated at 4 to 6x the fifth year's projected free cash flows depending upon market trends.

Clients often confuse market multiples of free cash flows with multiples applied to earnings per share and multiples of net profits. Needless to say, all three are different and will give different valuation results.

DCF is often used to estimate the value of intangibles where the asset backing is not significant.

Example68: DCF could be used to value franchise rights, territory rights, goodwill, leases [long leases for which premiums may be receivable on surrender or transfer], brand names, process patents. An aviation company would use DCF to value landing or air route rights.

In some instances and to some investors, all that matters for valuation, is the dividend distribution track record of a company or the earnings per share. Essentially, these investors would look at how quickly their investment would be recovered through dividends paid out by the company.

Example69: An investor may place a higher value on a share of Relgate which may have a dividend of 98% of the face value of shares versus shares of Mazon which does not declare dividends as a policy. Although he may have purchased the share of Mazon at a higher price premium.

Conversely,

Example70: An investor may value his shares in a web based B2B business, which does not declare dividends, at a higher premium, than an investment in a stable milk/ cheese products or transport company. The investor may be valuing the web based business on the prospect/ potential of high growth in the share price in the near future. This expectation of higher share price may be due to an expectation of higher profits or simply due to an expectation of higher speculative upward pressure on the B2B business' share price. People were willing to buy Lacebook's shares initially at $45 as they expected speculative pressure to push up the share price to much higher levels [although not justified by profitability or dividends].

However, a company not declaring dividends represents a higher risk for the investor as the investor can only hope to make a profit if the value of the share rises after funds reinvested in the business show profitable returns. Some companies in the USA in their filings with the SEC at the time of raising funds clearly specify their intentions of distributing or not distributing dividends to shareholders.

In industries where the cost structure, both controllable and non-controllable costs, is well predictable, and the depreciation/ amortization number is either not material or predictable, a suitable methodology for valuation is a multiple of net profits. This assumes that the business is optimally managed and there no restructuring costs.

Example71: A home furnishings and home accessories, OmsRUs, single box store would be usefully valued at a multiple of net profits, if at least 4 years financial statements are available for review. Exceptional, one-off items impacting the net profits of OmsRUs, should be excluded if these are non-recurring.

Example72: A large one-time settlement payment with a trade union should be added back, a one-time rebate from a large supplier should be deducted from profits declared as a non-recurring item, one-time costs relating to a lawsuit should be added back etc. before arriving at the level of sustainable net profits to which a multiple may be applied.

Some firms, because their activities follow a different business model can be valued on basis [market based multiples] such as:

(a) Eyeballs for a web platform
(b) Eyeballs per page for specific pages

(c) Number of clicks on pages with products or services offered for sale

(d) Number of billable hours in a legal firm

(e) Amount of VAT payments on production by a steel or cement or textile plant

(f) Different multiples for number of in-patients, number of emergency patients, day surgeries and clinic consultation visits

(g) Number of short stay business travelers and number of tourist passengers with at least a week's stay

(h) Amount of low interest or interest free deposits by a retail bank. A retail bank catering to a district with shipping companies could end up have a large amount of low or even interest free current account balances on a regular basis

(i) Number of connections for a cable or internet service provider or number of files of salaried individuals/ small businesses with a tax accountant

(j) Number of repeat programs or reprints of a media software production house and a publishing firm

During a valuation process, the consultant is required to make several assumptions, also represent financial numbers, develop projections [although in some instances management may provide these projections], make assumptions about terminal values and discount rate, assume a rate of growth of sales revenues etc. The consultant is also required to make judgments regarding the sustainability and quality of revenues, the incidence of defaults etc. The valuation process is finally dependent upon the best judgment of the person's carrying out the valuation [this is so even under IFRS based valuations]. Valuations are therefore, best carried out by persons who have expert knowledge of the relevant sector. Valuations carried out by generalists, will typically have several limitations, rely largely on assumptions provided by management, and will be merely, arithmetical exercises with workings provided in MS Excel.

Example73: A consultant [or members on his team] would need specialized knowledge [and past experience] for valuation of schools, telecom companies, banks, investment companies, food retailers, hotels, steel or cement manufacturing units, open cast or underground mines etc. Each of these would have distinct business and sector issues which affect profitability and future growth aspects. Not all of the business specific issues would be discernible from published sources or from the financials. The rate of working capital increases and cash flow generation, the terminal values and discount rates would differ very significantly for each sector.

A large and profitable valuation practice in North America is valuations in the event of divorce proceedings [presumably no goodwill is involved].

4.8 Statistics

Every consultant and aspiring consultant needs to be able to use appropriately basic statistical techniques, to arrive at more accurate conclusions. This is particularly true in cases where the consultant is required to analyse and draw conclusions from large volumes of data:

(i) Sampling techniques
(ii) Measures of average, mean, median and mode
(iii) Measures of deviation
(iv) Regression and correlation

These basic statistical techniques are fairly easy to understand and apply in the real world.

They help to explain how variables behave over time and the relationship between variables. These techniques Very useful in predicting values of variables.

Example74: The study of the causes of industrial accidents may reveal a specific cause and effect relationship or a random occurrence. The study of defaults and bankruptcy cases within a credit portfolio may reveal specific factors that can predict such defaults, such as consistently overdrawn or unpaid balances and long outstanding creditor balances. The study of accidents at a construction site may reveal a trend and specific causes.

Example75: Statistically a firm may document product defects, reasons for returns from customers and reasons for product rejections. A magazine subscription and distribution firm may analyze why customers have returned copies and discontinued the subscriptions. A restaurant chain may analyze data on consumer spending during different times of the day and data on which items are sold more often to which groups of customers. This would help in the process of menu engineering.

Example76: An airline company may review the impact of a planned increase in prices as compared with lower bookings during a season. If there is no/ little reduction and demand is not elastic, the airline may profitably increase prices up to a level. If the demand is sensitive to pricing of competitor and changes in pricing by competitors, then a proper statistical analysis would reveal the extent of correlation. The impact of marketing campaigns could be assessed and related to short term and longer term increases of sales of products being marketed/ advertised.

Example77: A ferrous alloys [input to steel production] or cement or glass producer may review the types of quality or defects in production batches in relation to the source of ore or fluctuations in electricity during production. Production defects may be more prevalent during production runs for batches using ore from a particular source, or production runs may have more defects during a particular work shift.

Example78: A retail finance company may statistically analyse incidences of defaults in payments [delays or absolute defaults] across various types and segments of customers e.g. salaried individuals, senior managers, shop floor or store workers, professionals such as doctors/ accountants/ engineers, small businessmen, start up business owners, location [city]. Customers below or above a certain salary income may have a lower/ higher incidence of defaults and/ or delays in payment of instalments. Customers from a particular industry who have served as employees for less than 5 years may have had a poorer track record for repayments.

Example79: A personal soaps or personal care shampoo or cream producer may statistically analyse the severity and period for which sales drop whenever a competitor product is launched. A large well established hotel or restaurant may statistically analyse similarly, by how much and for how long revenue falls when a competitor opens up with a specific catchment area/ radius of say a mile and a half.

Example80: A fast food chain may analyse by how much overall sales have fallen in a territory by taking off then menu a localized signature item temporarily.

Statistical techniques are used to establish cause and effect relationships between variables, in order to precisely define the root cause of problems, and then, accordingly design and implement solutions. Statistical techniques provide fact based and logical evidence, which is more reliable and has greater credibility than relying on individual/ team 'gut' feel.

Given the right motivation, a statistician can probably prove anything in the universe.

4.9   Consulting Proposals

"That's not bad. But most of the other consultants gave us mission statements with a bit more detail."

Consulting proposals take various forms. A proposal could be submitted in a template or an MS Word document or by email. Contractually, a proposal constitutes an offer and the acceptance of the proposal [offer] forms a contract between the client and the consultant. This contract results in the following obligations on the consultant, in exchange for the agreed fee:

(a) Assigning specific staff to the project as committed in the proposal
(b) Using the committed methodology and approach to the project
(c) Completing the specified scope of work as given in the proposal
(d) Completing specific deliverables within the required time frame for draft and final deliverables in the language required [translated if local language is a requirement]

(e) Making a presentation or having a discussion on the final deliverable including recommending mode and time frame for implementation

The proposal should be tailored to the recipient. A proposal for a large corporation would differ from a proposal to a small entrepreneur. A proposal to an entrepreneur would be more personalized, more dependent upon the individuals involved and the objective of building a longer term relationship.

The consultant in fact does face an important choice right up front. When to issue a proposal? A successful consultant knows when to pass an opportunity and when to deliver a proposal. An invitation to submit a proposal may be declined any of the following reasons:

(a) Scope of work is outside the capabilities of the consultant/s team or the scope involves complexities and effort which the consultant/s team does not want to undertake at this point in time

(b) The consultant does not have the appropriate staff for a project of this nature and quality would be compromised

(c) There are limitations on the availability of data, information e.g. benchmarking information may not be available

(d) The client is restricting access to some critical internal data e.g. a client may restrict access to a period of inventory records or a period of bank statements or bank statements for a specific bank account

(e) The project fee is likely to be un remunerative, resulting in a loss for the client and additional project fees do not compensate in the longer term

(f) The client has a strong preference and relationship with another consultant and is merely seeking competitive quotes to establish a baseline price

A good proposal should include the following:

(i) A fee that ensures the client will realize value for services provided. Ideally, the consultant's services should pay for itself

(ii) A detailed understanding of the project background and the scope

(iii) Credentials of similar projects carried out successfully

(iv) Testimonials from past clients

(v) An established methodology and approach for the project. This is particularly important in a competitive scenario. For example the proposal for valuation of a business could rely on different methodologies some of which may not be practical, may not be acceptable to the client or may result in an overly low valuation of the business [e.g. net adjusted asset value]

(vi) Clearly defined deliverables which crystallize value for the client consistently and at as early a stage as possible.

Example81: A consultant is developing policies and procedures for a client. S/he should have milestones on a project, including interviewing relevant staff, draft designs of systems/ templates, discussion of draft processes etc. It is a terrible idea to turn up after say, 8 weeks, and show up with a policies and procedures manual that has not seen rounds of discussions with the client, thus lacking in client ownership of the deliverable.

Example82: A consultant is required to develop an organization structure and a valuation report. S/he turns up after 8 weeks with the deliverable. The consultant has relied on industry standards [leading practices] and has not discussed with the client the aims/ objectives of the project and the pros and cons of various approaches. The client finds the deliverables irrelevant and distant from ground reality. The assumptions to the valuation report have not been discussed as well and the client finds that the growth rate and discount rate assumptions used are inappropriate.

(vii) Time frame for the project and milestones to measure progress. Often payments are also agree upon in line with progress milestones

Example83: A typical fee payment schedule would include 25%/ 30% or 50% in advance depending upon the consultant's risk assessment. An advance fee is required to ensure the client's commitment to the project. Subsequent payments may be based upon milestones such as completing interviews with management/ collecting required data, submission of draft report, discussion of draft report, finalization of draft report after client feedback.

It is always important to specify time limits for client feedback for responses to the draft deliverables, and to ensure that each milestone invoice is paid in full before proceeding to the next stage. Collecting a receivable for deliverables already delivered in full can often be a heart wrenching experience for the individual, non-big brand consultant team.

(viii)   Resumes of the staff that will actually carry out the project.

Example84: The proposed consultant CVs should be of the requisite seniority, and qualifications. For example a team for a telecom project or a consulting project for a bank should have relevant experience in that sector. At the proposal stage the consultant team committed to the project may have to make a competitive presentation to the client before selection. A consultant team pitching for a strategy project for a commercial bank would stand a low chance of success if the proposed project team members have had no actual exposure to the workings of a commercial bank, not being ex bank employees of reasonable seniority, or not having carried out successfully a similar project previously.

(ix) Resources and technology tools available as required within the consulting network.

Example85: A consultant firm setting out to do a benchmarking/ cost reduction/ process improvement exercise for a construction/ textile business unit could refer to its proprietary database of key performance indicators accumulated over the years by providing various services to other clients in the same sector, whether within the same geography or not. An internal audit consultant may be a knowledge pack of typical observations/ findings/ cost reduction/ efficiency issues in the particular industry, built up over time through sharing of knowledge with other offices in other cities or countries.

Perhaps the most important is the CVs of the staff which would be assigned to and available for the project. A preliminary scoping meeting could be arranged for the client to interact with the planned project team. This would enable the client to get a feeling of the value which the consultant could deliver on the project through business insights.

Correct scoping and understanding of the objectives of the project is critical. This enables appropriate selection of methodologies and approach, better estimation of costs and fees. Correct scoping should also include the specification of exclusions so as to allow for additional billing for extensions of the scope. A large number of consulting proposals fail in achieving selection because of incomplete or inadequate understanding of the client's needs.

Example86: A client SPDC, wants a fair valuation of its various loans to small businesses. These businesses set up in different sectors are not asset heavy, but were intended to develop either retail businesses or intellectual property through software systems and aps. The consultant incorrectly assumes that the client needs the valuation in order to refinance its portfolio and proposes a net asset valuation [which in this case would give the lowest possible value for the start-ups].

Example87: A client Ghnemic, has requested a valuation of its various business divisions. The client wants the valuation to present to a potential private equity investor for the purpose of acquiring a minority stake. The consultant assumes that the purpose of the valuation is to submit a valuation report to the banks/ lending financial institutions or for purposes of internal performance evaluation.

Example88: A proposal for a business valuation may exclude the technical valuation of fixed assets, as this may not be as relevant as the earnings potential of these assets. A proposal for a feasibility study may exclude preparation of an information memorandum/ cash flow plan or monthly budgets. A proposal for developing an organization structure may include job descriptions for only the key management positions and may not include incentive schemes.

A consultant should propose for what s/he can deliver at a cost at which he can make a reasonable profit. There is little point in pricing the proposal low enough to succeed in selection if the project does not result in a profit for the consultant.

Consulting proposals may follow different pricing models:

(a) Fixed fee e.g. for designing an organization structure or delivering a feasibility report

(b) Success on completion of the project. Examples are for assisting with establishment of a new company or division or hotel, setting up an eCommerce division or active social media marketing team, establishing a risk management function, delivering a valuation report, or increasing the issued share capital

(c) Success fee dependent on results of a project: Examples are funds raised for a project on the basis of an information memorandum, cost reduction achieved, number of new retail finance clients generated by a change in marketing policy/ tactics, new contracts signed for additional business, increased sales etc. For example, in the early days ERP firms charged large automotive major's success fees on the basis of additional units produced from a specific manufacturing location. A consultant should obviously, not accept a fee arrangement for a valuation project, where the amount of fee is dependent upon the amounts at which the client is valued

(d) Hourly charge out rates for each level of staff depending on seniority and skill sets [engineering design, architectural, financial/ budgeting, legal associates, a legal firm's partner time].

(e) A mix of the above

(f) A fee dependent upon a competitor or supplier surrendering a benefit to the company [e.g. an aviation competitor withdrawing from a particular route, a supplier paying a volume rebate after negotiations].

(g) Timing of payment of fees. As mentioned earlier above, an advance is usually recommended with balances payable on submission of draft report and balance on submission of final report & presentation. This would differ according to the consultant's assessment of the client appetite and risk profile in each case.

Proposals are usually competitive and are often required to be supported by in person presentations and discussions on the methodology and approach, past experiences etc. These discussions enable the consultant to better understand the scope of work and enable the client to appreciate the consultant team, methodology and approach.

Pricing [consultant's fees] could be:

(a) Full costs price
(b) Lower price because of repeat projects from the same client
(c) Lower price because the profile of the client enables future marketing to others in the same industry
(d) Higher price because of particularly challenging circumstances, delays anticipated in client's approval of deliverables [often the case with governmental companies] and difficult locations [poor infrastructure or extreme climatic conditions]
(e) Lower price because the consultant needs market share and recognition for that type of project

(f) Higher price because the consultant knows that the client has a limited choice of consultants for this type of project

(g) Lower price because the consultant has full time team members who are already guaranteed minimum payments and have spare chargeable hours, and there are competing firms.

A consultant's pricing model needs to include [and demonstrate] a minimum of overhead charges [expensive office, high expenses on printing/binding of deliverables] which do not directly add value to the client's business or the client's understanding of the deliverables.

Example89: A consultant firm XDO may have been engaged to develop a financial model and feasibility of a multipurpose retail development. The consultant may deliver the final output by way of:

(a) A hard copy report, in English and a translated version in the local language

(b) An email submission

(c) A presentation to the client

(d) A financial model in soft copy

(e) A graphical presentation of the layout of the site as fully developed including holograms and video with walkthrough images

(f) All of the above

Don't give away too much in the proposal, else the client may attempt an in house solution.

4.10   Value Engineering

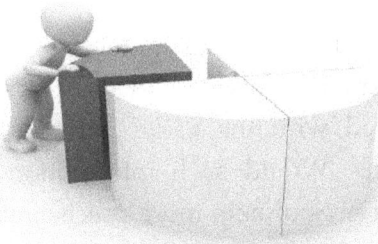

Value engineering can be usefully applied to products and processes. Value engineering involves the measurement of costs [direct and indirect] and comparison with time and/or value dynamics. These dimensions can be represented graphically, or in tables or critical path method diagrams [CPM/ PERT]

Example90: The cost of an extra coat of paint. Value delivered can be worked out by the additional price that the buyer is willing to pay. This can be compared with the additional costs of:

(a) Labour hours
(b) Material costs
(c) Machine hour time/ paint shop time

(d) Additional inventories required of paint materials, other consumables and the finished product as drying would take additional time

Example91: The cost of gathering information about customers or about arrivals at an airport can be compared with the value derived from such information. Would such information assist the security services of help more precise marketing of goods and services within the terminal? Is such information gathering really relevant. In recent years, a number of countries/ terminals have made the foreign immigration control cards simple one pagers and have done away with landing cards for nationals. Of course if you are Facebook, all information has a value.

Example92: Alternative processes within a Finance or HR department would have different costs and value delivered. An automated/ on line process would have different value dimensions from a manually delivered process e.g. a retail banking service. A company may track attendance through:

(a) Punched attendance cards
(b) Finger swiping
(c) Facial or eye lens recognition devices

(d) Signed off time sheets [automated or manual]

(e) Attendance registers [manual or on line clock ins]

Each alternative would have different costs, time and value [some alternatives may simultaneously record other information]. A loyalty card system may include:

(a) A simple personal show of a card and thereby purchase at a discount

(b) A card with a magnetic strip and photo, the magnetic strip permitting recording of history of the customer's purchases and charge to the customer's designated bank account.

A careful study would lead to a recommendation about inputs/ process or time based on incremental value delivered through different routes.

Example93: A table or ceiling fan producer GFL can value engineer his product based on number of blades/ ball bearings/ copper winding on the motor/ weight of the blades, size of the motor etc. Price, customer perception of value, raw material input costs and production processing costs would be reviewed in relation to each variable. A lower cost ['cheaper'] input for example may mean higher processing time for a production batch and more rejections on the production line, also more labour hours as a result of additional manual processes.

Example94: A value engineered loan application approval or marketing process by a retail finance company may involve more automation, less personal intervention, quicker processing, and lower incidence of defaults or delayed payments. A Russian human resources consulting company has developed a robot for hiring employees. The robot carries out simultaneously hundreds of calls, schedules interviews, administers online cultural fit and technical proficiency tests and short lists candidates for personal interviews based on predetermined benchmark scores. This was applied to oil & gas firms [downstream and upstream], banking and telecom clients.

Example95: A value engineered process of preliminary reviewing of patients at the emergency services of a hospital may lead to treating a higher number of patients, higher revenue and reduced waiting time for a patient to meet with the appropriate specialized consultant.

Value engineering usually requires flow charting of the process, meticulously plotting process step time, documents flows, approval processes and costs for each step. Value is usually worked out backward starting with the final selling price of the product, assigning to each process backwards to the beginning. The value engineering process is more insightful if the process steps to which value is assigned are broken down to the smallest possible step in the value chain.

Example96: A customer purchases boxes of rubber gaskets. Each box has ten gaskets and ten boxes are packed in a larger box. The firm GasX adds $2 to the price for the larger box of ten boxes. Each box is sold individually for $14 and the larger box is sold for $142. GasX should identify the material cost of the larger box, the machine hours needed to pack batches in larger boxes, the labour cost of such large box packing, the time needed and then compare this with the $2 charge. It may well turn out that the reduced cost of delivery for the larger boxes may more than offset the additional costs of putting together the larger boxes. The material cost, machine hours and labour costs can be broken down into smaller steps such as ordering, storing, maintaining equipment, recruiting, training etc.

Example97. A consultant may develop and/ or use complex software for monitoring time recorded on various consulting projects, on a daily/ weekly basis. A review may show that such tracking reduced valuable consulting time and adds no value to the client. Consultants may instead simply email at the end of every week or even month, time spent on projects, especially if the number of projects being worked on in parallel is not more than, say, 4 projects.

The natural and logical position of value engineering is customer focus. Anything else and it would sit uncomfortably beside other ill conceived management initiatives.

4.11 Authority Matrix

Authority Vs Responsibility

Every organization, whether profit of non-profit, business or religious or charitable, should have an authority matrix [AM]. An AM specifies:

(i)   Authority
(ii)   Responsibility, and
(iii)   Accountability

For various organizational decisions such as:

(a) Purchasing and other routine operational decisions
(b) Hiring
(c) Capital expenditure
(d) Payments to suppliers of varying amounts, some large, some not so [large]
(e) Giving guarantees
(f) Opening bank accounts
(g) Paying out payroll
(h) Routine petty expenses
(i) Purchasing the rights to a brand
(j) Opening new companies etc.

Each AM should be structured top down from the Board of Directors, Governance committees [such as audit, compensation, investment, risk management etc.] to departments/ divisions [such as purchasing, marketing, human resources, finance, production, services, operations, quality control etc.]

An AM will typically cover:

  (a) Initiation
  (b) Review for comments
  (c) Approval
  (d) Executing and
  (e) Recording

Not all the above steps are applicable to each decision cycle or transaction.

AM should support segregation of duties. A single individual should not be responsible for initiation, review, approval and recording of transactions.

Example98: Functions/ authority which should typically be distributed between individuals:
  (a) Preparing bank transfers/ payment advices and reconciliation of bank accounts periodically should be separated. A large number of frauds have occurred due to lack of independent review of bank reconciliation statements
  (b) Selecting a supplier, approving the invoice, recording the invoice and processing the payment. Excess payments could be made,

advances may not be recovered or adjusted, fictitious invoices could be paid, if these functions are all with a single individual

(c) Making payments and comparing with budgetary approved limits

(d) Hiring personnel and processing payroll. This could lead to fictitious employees on the payroll. At a mine the mine manager should not have the authority to hire workers, determine bonus entitlements based on output, and process the payouts

(e) Approving leave/ increments and updating personnel records

(f) Setting KPIs and recording actual performance could lead to excess payments of bonus or incentives

(g) Opening customer remittances and recording the collections

(h) Using inputs in production, recording wastage and recording the quantity of inputs received from a supplier. Short receipts from a supplier could be paid for and passed off as production wastage.

Example99: A textile factory [production supervisor] may overstate the quantity of wool received, paying for excess quantities in cash. To adjust input output ratios which are regularly reported, the production supervisor [who was also responsible for paying for receipts of wool] would overstate production wastage and/ or overstate work in progress [which was eventually discovered as disproportionately high in comparison with finished production units]

(i) Servicing customers and recording customer complaints. Although more difficult to conceal in the days of social media accessible to all

(j) Hiring or terminating employees and recording exit interviews with leaving employees

(k) Collections of payments due [instalments] from customers and recording receivables and sending out reminders/ statements of account for receivables

(l) Production operations and sample testing of product quality in a pharmaceutical company

The purpose of segregation is simply to allow for independent operational control whist fixing responsibility points.

If more than one person is involved in a process there are significantly reduced chances of:

(a) Errors
(b) Inefficiencies
(c) Fraud as this would require collusion between 2 or more employees.

Example100: A payment process for company RKL requires an accountant to put together invoices due for payment after comparing it with the relevant purchase orders, and goods received note. The financial controller then reviews the invoice for budgetary approvals. The CFO approves the bank transfer letter for invoices up to $50,000 after checking the cash and bank position. For invoices above $50,000 the CFO and COO are required to jointly sign off the bank transfer [or cheque]. While a supplier may find the level of approvals time consuming, RKL has made it difficult for fictitious or un approved invoices to be paid or invoices to be paid out in excess of budgeted amounts, or bank transfers to be made when there are in sufficient funds available for payments.

Naturally, as may be expected, there are always objections to segregation of duties/ authority. Again, a sad feature of human nature. Everybody wants authority, few want responsibility and nobody wants accountability.

4.12 Succession Planning

Succession Planning [SP] is needed for all business firms whether family managed or professionally managed. SP ensures continuity of the organization's policies and in implementation of the vision and mission statements.

Business firms should develop effective second lines for all critical management functions. Second lines have to be diligently trained and prepared for the roles they are expected to eventually assume. Second lines do not occur by accident, rather through a conscious effort in selection and preparation.

Example101: A sports team CSK needs 11 playing team members. The team actually selects and prepares 16 team member, has a coach and an assistant coach, a manager and an assistant manager. Not having a second line leaves the team vulnerable to consistently fielding a high quality, well synchronized team. Key front line players may fall ill or may be injured during training or while playing or may be banned for a few games by the authorities.

Pitchforking individuals into management functions usually delivers poor results. Individuals should be selected and groomed, often multiple individuals for the same critical role. This means involving individuals in management decision making, negotiations, team building etc. Individuals so involved will gain familiarity with the implementation of the organization's policies, procedures and values.

Example102: A large organization my groom more than one divisional head to assume the role of chief executive officer or chief financial officer. The divisional heads, themselves would have deputies who could step into their shoes at relatively short notices. A central bank may groom more than one deputy governor for the role of governor. A military may groom more than one lieutenant general for the position of joint forces chief of staff.

Example103: A pharmaceutical company or a chemical company or a retail products company which relies exclusively on the professional/ technical product development skills of a particular individual, would do well to plan well in advance for the individual's retirement/ demise/ or exit to a competitor. Particularly so in the case of key production supervisors, key chemists or key marketing personnel who have significant day to day responsibilities. An architect's or a legal firm may be heavily reliant on the particular skills of one or few individuals. A single unplanned departure, may damage the future business prospects of the firm is a second line equally capable is not under development.

Preparing the appropriate second line is an ongoing process and usually takes several years even in family managed firms.

Coaching for a second line position usually involves formal management training and on the job training under a mentor or guide. In a family managed business the mentor may be the family patriarch of a senior family member. Training involves close coordination with the mentor so that the person being trained absorbs the methodologies, policies, ethics, values and commitment required for the position.

4.13 Profitability Improvement

Profitability improvement [PI] is often undertaken by business firms who want to improve their growth rate of internal accruals. A firm may aim to improve gross margin [ratio of direct costs (material, labour and machine) to sales], operating margin [after all expenses], return on assets, return on equity, return on human capital etc. Margins and expenses are reviewed in relation to the level of sales.

A consultant on a PI project would need to study the key cost elements and basis, their behaviour under different activity levels or patterns, how different commercial arrangements, or pricing would impact profitability.

Example104: A firm may consider the cost of outsourcing a maintenance or security or marketing or contact centre activity versus the investment of having the function in-house.

Example105: Ahlex may consider the cost of having an in house legal department versus outsourcing the activity to a legal firm for a predetermined number of retained hours per month. Similarly, with the book keeping function and the internal audit function. Some firms have 'interim' contracted CFOs during preparing the company for a public listing on a stock exchange or raising of capital through road show presentations to prospective investors.

Example106: A firm may consider increasing the price of a product. This may bring in additional revenue and may also reduce the number of sales transactions as fewer persons may purchase the firm's products. An increase in the selling price of a car by say, USD 2,000 may reduce the number of buyers for that model because customers have a choice of other car manufacturers.

Example107: A firm producing a fan may vary the quality of bearings thus reducing costs and the life of the motor. This reduction of costs may however lead to lower sales and perception of quality. On the other hand it could increase the number of repeat replacement sales. Chinese manufacturers target a lower selling price with lower quality so that replacement sales are high. Japanese car manufacturers realized early on that making cars which lasted for 20 years with minimum servicing was good for reputation but bad for sales and profits. They subsequently changed their business model to producing cars which ran efficiently for 3 to 5 years and then required expenditure on spare parts or replacement with a newer vehicle. Korean manufacturers adopted the same policy.

Example108: An installation of central copiers/ printers/ scanners on each floor would reduce the cost of individual printers but may add to capital and maintenance costs of the central printers. In addition the firm would incur the write off and disposal costs of the earlier printers if these cannot be surrendered for value to the new vendor of copier machines.

Example109: Automation at a factory production line may improve the throughput of the machines installed. An automated paint line is clearly far more productive on an assembly line. An automated croissant line or cupcake line may produce more quantities, with a standard taste profile, but not as artistically hand crafted. An automated car park check out with a slot machine or preloaded swipe cards may save on labour costs and may result in fewer missed charge opportunities, whilst adding on the costs of the software, hardware and the cards, although lost cards may be replaced for a fee. Automated production lines, unlike labour, do not pay taxes, do not incur labour insurance and benefits

PI projects could be rapid quick fixes focused on low hanging fruit, easy wins e.g. terminating non-value adding contracts outsourcing a delivery service.

Example110: A car servicing shop may focus on engine, brakes and other systems while profitably outsourcing external films, body repair jobs, paint jobs and periodic detailing to outsourced crews with an add on charge by the brand service agent.

PI projects could also be long winded detailed examination of processes or systems and all underlying cost elements and input costs of materials.

Example111: A chain of large restaurants in a PI project may examine the cost of all inputs for possible lower prices, rent arrangements with landlords, costs of distribution of products, the cost of establishing a central kitchen for common inputs, costs of overtime, costs of zero rated workers versus costs of monthly rated workers and training-hiring costs. It may then understand that some locations should be closed or downsized, at some locations space not utilized can be let out for sub tenancy rent, some grades of central kitchen production labour can be outsourced and made variable according to volumes. Association with a leading film star or Michelin star chef may bring in additional sales and better price premiums.

Example112: A hospital may review the profitability of various services e.g. plastic surgery, ophthalmology, nephrology, orthopaedic, cardiac etc. and determine whether some departments should be closed, relocated, expanded, outsourced [e.g. path lab, MRI] or supported by specialized surgery units [e.g. cathlab for angioplasty or angiograms ,or laser surgery for eyes or nuclear medicine tests for cardiac conditions] or even priced differently or need to be supported by additional medical consultants and surgeons. A hospital originally set up as a multi-specialty hospital may decide to focus on orthopaedic and cardiac specialties. Alternatively, a hospital originally set up as a specialty hospital may develop into a multi-specialty hospital with other departments.

Example113: A change in the product mix could result in lower number of sales units but higher sales revenue and higher profitability [not always the case]. A manufacturer of automobiles, orthopaedic equipment, personal care products or textiles may review demand and change the relative amounts of each product range/ product being produced. GCP manufactured a range of inks, pens, brushes and other personal writing instruments. A careful study of sales trends and accumulating inventories showed which colours, sizes and instruments [e.g. thin, medium or thick points] sold higher quantities and which sets delivered better production margins.

Example114: A retail finance company may shift from personal needs loans to loans for automobiles/ vehicles, education loans, medical expenses loans, vacation loans, house building loans, small business loans etc. with relevant regulatory approvals. This could be based on the estimated market demand for each loan, the estimated cost of marketing for such loan accounts, estimates of customer defaults and the basic gross margin on each loan product. Alternatively, the RFC may decide to shift from having a large number of smaller value loan accounts, to a fewer number of high value business loan accounts or to micro sized loans with a rural penetration focus which may have a significantly lower default rate and much higher compounded returns

Example115: A law firm may shift focus from personal/ criminal/ corporate/ transaction/ intellectual property rights or labour law practice. It may also shift focus from mainly providing commercial litigation services to providing legal services to business firms on a retainer ship basis.

Example116: A mining company AGRCT may understand that processing the ore and then selling the finished product may yield better profits even if the processing is outsourced to a third party, as compared with selling the ore. An oil company may understand that supplying oil to a refinery and then, in partnership, selling the refined product may yield more profits than selling crude oil to other refineries. An oil and gas company may realize that instead of investing more into new exploration, exploration rights may be let out in production partnership or joint venture structures.

Example117: A change in tax regulations may cause a chemicals trader or manufacturer to produce or trade in a different grade of chemicals. An automobile manufacturer may face higher or lower taxes on lower emission/ diesel/ electric vehicles and may change the production mix. Automobiles or vehicles with an engine capacity above 3ltrs or above 3 tonners in chassis weight may be subject to higher or lower taxes depending upon governmental policy.

Example118: A food distribution company may realize that distributing locally/ own produced or sourced brands of organic food results in much better margins [albeit lower sales volumes] than trading in high volume low margin [after royalties] branded products. The lower sales volumes may be more than offset by or may not be offset by the higher per unit prices. A poor step to improve profitability would be to reduce essential processing steps thereby reducing product quality below safe levels or reducing packed quantity [below what is mentioned on the packing labeling and what the customer is paying for].

Example119: A hotel may improve profitability by going eco-friendly in terms of waste recycling, lower wattage lighting, better aircon systems, rooftop solar energy, own grown organic vegetables, distribution to charitable organizations of excess prepared and raw food inputs [e.g. fruits, rice, wheat before the projected expiry dates]. In addition, the eco friendly hotel may attract more customers who are environment conscious and may also quote a higher room tariff.

Example120: A steel company SAR, could reduce power consumption by reducing consumption during batch changes e.g. not running empty furnaces for long periods. An aviation company can reduce fuel consumption by ensuring that pilots adhere to the optimum flight path [every deviation costs money], and that aircraft at terminals are using generators and not aviation fuel to power up systems and air-conditioning. The steel company SAR could eliminate some products with small volumes and requiring live furnace changeovers. The aviation company eliminated some routes and added some routes both nationally and internationally. The aviation company decided to carry on some more domestic routes because it was then entitled by the national aviation regulatory body, to fly on certain much more profitable international routes to London, Toronto, San Jose, JFK.

Profitability improvement is always a challenge because elected governments find new ways to levy taxes and enlarge the tax base to fund populist schemes in their never attempt to purchase votes. Every dollar to the government is a dollar out of the shareholders' pockets.

4.14   Process Reengineering

Process reengineering [PRe] is usually fundamentally changing a process to deliver better quality results faster. Textbook consultants like to use the word 'paradigm' shift, but then many consultants are terribly attached to their pet jargon. Processes over time become cumbersome. Organizations as they grow, add on layers of internal operational controls, documentation, approvals and financial controls to ensure integrity of transactions. This however, leads to delays and time spent on processing transactions.

Example121: Macroon is a business firm letting out sea side chalets. It is a 56 year old firm. Payments above $1,500 are processed through five individuals, most of whom initial or sign without checking anything and merely rely on the signature of the previous individual. Further, although the company has implemented an ERP solution, Macroon retains most analysis and schedules on MS Excel worksheets and MS Power point presentations, prints daily an estimated one ton of paper documents which are available on the system.

Example122: An organization may need too much time to authorize and issue a purchase order for items which are regularly sold in large quantities directly to customers. Worldwide large grocery, spare parts and other retailing firms are using AI [artificial intelligence or programs] to place automated orders based on sales trends and inventory holding, allowing for minimum inventory holding, no stock outs and no or minimum date expired stock.

PRe often, though not always, involves automation or the use of computer software, even apps on mobile phones.

Example123: Retail banks in Kenya have long since joined hands with telecom companies to enable quick transfers and penetration into rural, agriculture based societies. This has also enabled micro finance type lending in Kenya, Zimbabwe and other parts of Africa and Asia.

Example 124: In the UK, many firms have set up direct debit arrangements with their suppliers. The suppliers invoices based on credit terms are directly debited to the bank accounts without need for time consuming approval processes e.g. British Gas, regular and reliable supplies to a retail chain/ supermarket of daily inventory items.

PRe usually commences with meticulously drawing a flow chart of the process. The transaction initiation process, comparison steps, the approval process, documentation, recording, archiving etc. The flow chart is supplemented by sample documents at each stage with all their copies [often several copies in white, blue, yellow, green colours]. Flow charts may have colour codes depending upon the criticality of the process, process bottlenecks, time and costs and constraints.

A reduction in steps may be a reduction in number of copies, a reduction in number of approval steps or reduction in unnecessary retention of copies at intermediate stages [especially of documents are stored on-line within computer databases]. Even a reduction in storage/ retention of documents is a process improvement.

Many organizations not having a detailed document retention process end up storing huge volumes of mainly unwanted documents, files and correspondence.

While implementing PRe a consultant should be careful that essential internal operational controls or financial controls are not eliminated entirely or even unnecessarily diluted. It may look unnecessary to compare payment requisitions the budget limits, however, lack of budgetary control could result in financial disaster and a nasty surprise in the year end audited financial statements.

Example125: Quicker processing of payments should not by pass the pre-approval step of comparison with approved budgets. Quicker issue of high value purchase orders should not by pass the important step of obtaining comparative quotes. Recruitment processes should not by pass the relevant technical or culture scan tests. An organization did not track development expenses of a new brand versus originally approved budgets [by the Board]. At the year-end it was discovered that the new brand's development expenses [which are required to be charged to the income statement for the year under international financial reporting standards] had completely offset the profits of the continuing operations.

Example126: A recruitment process was changed to allow department heads to hire non managerial personnel without reference to the technical and culture scan software tests [minimum scores]. This resulted in a large number of unusually early separations [resignations or exits], more frequent recruitments, process instability, higher legal costs [exits], and higher recruitment costs.

There are several flow charting techniques available. The most common convention is for the chart to follow the logical sequence of the process from top left of the page to bottom right. The flow chart is also usually split vertically into departments, for easy understanding of how documents, information and knowledge flow from one department/ function to the other. Flow charting convention usually has different symbols for documents to be approved, retained [filed], discarded, sent to another department, scanned for database retention etc.

Example127: A flow chart to order a replenishment of inventory may commence from a requisition by the inventory controller to the purchasing department [issue of the purchase order] to the finance and accounting functions [receipt of the supplier's invoice, payment to the supplier and recording the inventory].

Take away all the jargon and PRe simply means better balance and alignment between:

(a) Customer requirements
(b) Value delivered by the process versus costs of the process steps
(c) Time required for the process [this is important to the customer and also incurs costs for the producer/ supplier]
(d) Price charged either as down payment of deferred payment to the customer

Typically, as a rule of thumb, the smaller the process is broken down into steps, the more the possibilities of identifying opportunities for Pre leading to cost or time reduction or increases in revenue or value.

Example129: A change in distribution scheduling may require the firm to hold either more or less inventory and conversely for distributors or customers. More inventory holding by the original manufacturer [OEM] could mean lower inventory holding for distributors e.g. critical or expensive spares. Conversely, a vehicle manufacturer, say of heavy duty earth moving vehicles/ equipment may not hold inventory and may require distributors in each territory to hold finished units inventory.

Example130: A change in quality control procedures to check for certain defects at earlier stages may eliminate further processing costs on production units which would be rejected at a later stage. A textile manufacturing unit, rejects certain below par batches at a very early stage before combing and colour integration operations, thus saving on wastage of material, labour and machine hours.

Example131: The processing of ready mix concrete within the vehicle while on route reduces holding and delivery time. In the case ships exporting product from Japan or Korea to the USA, several finishing production steps are carried out on the way for clothes and cars. Clothes arrive at the final destination in containers on racks as they need to be inserted and displayed finally in the retail stores.

Example132: Reengineering of a product using a lower cost critical raw material reduces the price to the customer, thus increasing sales. It also often lowers the life of the product thus leading to repeat sales. It is basically not good business to produce a long lasting product unless it is a brand which commands a premium price.

Example133: Reengineering a hospital's emergency services by using in some instances telemedicine or apps would lead to quicker response times and better use of expensive consultant hours which are in limited supply.

Example134: Publishing a book or even writing a book may involve different authors or editors working simultaneously on different sections of the manuscript of the book and then having a senior editor/s merging the works together. A book on accountancy may have two or more co-authors contributing online from different countries with a senior editor ensuring quality and continuity of style, standard of material etc to deliver a uniform experience to the reader.

PRe could either involve rapid impact small trims to a process [e.g. eliminating a copy of a purchase order or eliminating a step in approval of payments], or a significant change in process [e.g. online approvals and payments of suppliers invoices, system generated reorders of stock items based on predetermined stock levels using AI, customer orders received through an outsourced call centre or through mobile phone apps, the call centre being located in another country].

Example135: Company Effex required two signatures for cheques to suppliers if the amount of the cheque was above $2,000. One signature from Finance and the other from Operations. This inevitably led to delays since both signatories were often not simultaneously available and the incidence of such cheques was large. Considerable improvement was witnessed by simply allowing the CFO to be sole signatory for all cheques up to $8,000. A print run of payments released by the CFO was passed daily for information to the COO [as a matter of internal control]. A relatively minor effort change resulted in a huge process improvement without any appreciable dilution of controls or efficiency.

Example134: A company Protex produces a goat's and camel milk product at a dairy. It later at the retail unit adds cheese powder and/ or cream to some units based on customer's requirements. This caters to some customers, however, the consumption of cheese and cream is uneven, often more than standard, and is not fully compensated for by the increase in sales price added on for customers choosing the cheesy creamy option. Protex now saves cheese & cream input costs and fully recovers its costs through increased selling price. Protex shifted to a system of producing some batches of cheese & cream coated products at the production point itself, producing to a formula, packing and labeling the premium batches for sale at a higher price. Sales revenues increased through proper pricing to the customers, improved branding, enhanced customer perception of quality control and standardization, whereas the costs of cheese & cream relative to the quantity sold reduced.

Example136: Implementing of Sharepoint platform and sharing individual calendars enabled a company Yaas to significantly improve the utilization of time of senior executives and reduce instances of conflicting meeting times, prompt sharing of draft documents in collaborative development modes e.g. project plans, product designs, workshop or mega store designs.

4.15 Risk Management

Risk Management [RM] includes the following:

(a) Identification of strategic, operational, business specific, and market risks.
(b) Measurement of risks
(c) Risk monitoring on a periodic or ongoing basis
(d) Risk mitigation and avoidance measures and maintenance of a risk ledger

Example137: The risk that a competitor will replicate the product with more features and a lower cost e.g. a mobile phone design a software app. A high degree of such a risk would limit the amount that the company is willing to invest in the development.

Example138: The financial risk of borrowing too much and operations not generating sufficient profits to repay the loans. A new business in a highly competitive market for producing moulded furniture may set up sites and marketing campaigns in different geographies based on an optimistic expansion plan. Sales may be lower than estimated leading to shortfalls in the cash flows required to repay or even service the loans.

Example139: The risk of a production unit being overly dependent on a single source of raw material or component supplier or a restaurant being overly dependent on the master chef. The risk of not protecting the intellectual property rights to a product or process design. A manufacturer of electronic items needs rare earth minerals and these are sourced from one particular country in Africa. A political or security disturbance results in abrupt termination of the supply chain. A food trading firm sources a high quality grade of basmati rice from a particular supplier in Gujarat, India. An unusual delay in monsoon, results in crop failure and inadequate inventory to support sales targets. A mobile phone producer invents a device which uses a solar powered/ chargeable battery and a phone which does not need an Intel chip. A competitor replicates the technology within 2 months of launch thus limiting any competitive advantage, whilst spending less than a third on development expenses.

Risk management could involve insurance which is essentially sharing the risk with a larger body of firm facing a similar risk. Risks could be shared between producers in the same sector [e.g. dairy farmers, poultry farmers supporting each other by co-insurance from loss of livestock due to illness or infection]. Diamond traders from loss of inventory due to theft in transit.

Risk avoidance could simply mean not undertaking certain activities that are high risk.

Example140: Portfolio risk may be diversified by investing in fixed income bearing securities and also in different equities in different sectors or in firms at different stages of their business cycle. Portfolio risk is greatly increased by investing a major portion in equities and in a particular sector or a particular company's equity. Portfolio risks could also be minimized by investing at different points of the index to allow for cyclical variations. The investor could invest in a mix of high risk high return instruments and relatively lower risk, lower return instruments. An investor could invest in bonds available at different discounts, in different currencies, with different maturity dates, with different credit risk rated companies in different countries [e.g. investments in the Euro could be split between several countries].

It is important to measure, monitor and grade risks regularly. It is unwise for an organization to let risks accumulate and build up without constant monitoring. Year-end snapshots are not a good practice as there could be significant build-up of risks in the intervening 12 months. A simple example below to demonstrate that many risks require active monitoring and regular measurement.

Example141: A large steel company SRsteel has seven different bank accounts and pays out thousands of bank transfers and cheques each month, some of which are in different currencies. The new MBA head of finance believes it is not necessary and in fact plain inconvenient to carry out bank reconciliations at the end of each month for each of the seven bank accounts. SRsteel therefore discontinues the automated matching of banking transactions booked versus the bank statements and the corresponding reconciliations. At the end of the year, the year-end closing process at 31st December, the bank balance confirmations and the audit process, reveals that there was a banking fraud committed in the month of May. The employee has since left SRsteel with all of his dues and his whereabouts are not known.

Example142: A commercial bank DBK's retail branch is required to reconcile teller and bank cash balances at the end of each day. There is a long national holiday with festivities from Friday to Monday. On Tuesday, DBK's branch discovers through reconciliation now carried out that over $2mn is missing and was probably disbursed across the counter. Review of the tapes confirms this and the passing on of cash by the teller to his spouse across the counter and refilling from the safe. The teller and spouse had left the country on Thursday night through a series of connecting flights, and are not traceable despite Interpol notices.

Example143: A food trading company Fresh Lobster sells goods on credit and receives at the time of shipment post-dated cheques for the value of shipments. The cheques are typically deposited a month after the shipment, allowing for the credit period. The firm does not have a procedure of monthly bank reconciliation statements and notices from banks are routinely filed. The firm discovers six months later that the past 4 month's cheques have been returned unpaid. The customer is no longer traceable, has moved to a nearby country and Fresh Lobster has to write off $257,000 of non-recoverable debts.

Example144: A central production unit dispatches finished units of hardware in various SKUs to a subsidiary in a different country. The local management and the CPU monitors the subsidiaries reconciliation of goods received, sales and inventory in the warehouse. However, for the past 6 months, the new manager at the CPU has not reconciled the quantity despatched to the subsidiary with their records. The subsidiary [warehouse manager] under reports quantities received but reconciles these short quantities with its sales and inventory. These reconciliations are provided to local management and to the CPU. The warehouse manager has been under recording receipts from the CPU in his systems, the excess inventory has been sold in the local market by the warehouse manager at a discount. The SKU unit

125

price is $350 and in the in four months, the CPU lost $437,500 in sales value.

The likelihood of a risk event occurring usually varies inversely with the potential severity of the actual impact. Highly likely risk events usually have a lower potential impact.

Example145: The risk that a large, reputed company with a good credit rating will default has a low likelihood. However, in the event of default the loss to the supplier could be huge because of the larger credit limits set. A manufacturer in the EU, Tedco supplies ToyR with a large quantity of children's' toys on a monthly basis. These are expensive toys which are compliant with various input regulations applicable to children's toys. The credit limit was set over twelve years back at four months' outstanding. ToyR declares bankruptcy and closes all of its stores. Tedco now has difficulty getting 50cents to the $ on all of its outstanding invoices aggregating to $1.625mn, as the outstanding invoices were a little over 4 months' supplies and the red flag on the poor payment record was not raised on a timely basis within Tedco.

Example146: A family managed business ASaya had given a general manager Gitesh, a broad power of attorney, years back to represent them generally and very broadly with franchisors, bankers and regulatory authorities. After serving for 23 years, the Gitesh retires, unfortunately, not exiting ASaya on good terms. The power of attorney has not been canceled. The general manager transfers a key franchise to his own company, and takes a bank loan by mortgaging the assets of ASaya. ASaya is engaged in a lengthy legal battle which will probably continue for years. ASaya has a crippled business until the outcome of the Court proceedings and Gitesh has a flourishing family business of his own with the brand and funding of ASaya.

It is important for all organizations to maintain a risk ledger. A risk ledger records risks which have been recognized by management, states the decisions taken to measure, monitor, manage or avoid risks. Specific decisions should be taken to manage risks and to take remedial and/ or protection steps when risk events to occur. Risk mitigation measures usually need to be taken swiftly when a risk occurs.

Most organizations believe that risk management is for banks, financial institutions and investment companies. It is important to recognize that all organizations face risks from the business environment in which they operate. All business involves risks and organizations need to ensure that the consequences of such risks are more than offset by the profits from such business ventures.

Example147: A multi-national holding company Abexco operates across several business and product groups in various countries. Abexco is vulnerable to the following risks:

(a) Risks of currency fluctuation and devaluation of currency in countries which are not either politically or economically stable

(b) Increases in direct or indirect taxes in various countries

(c) Lack of adequate and timely control over operations of subsidiaries

(d) General powers of attorney given to heads of strategic business units in various countries

(e) Risk of competition by way of market entry of a major competitive brand or a new brand

(f) Risk of change in government resulting in cancelation of contracts. Business firms have been knows to lose large amounts in countries such a Pakistan, Iraq, Egypt, African countries on change of government, since the successor government may disavow the previously signed agreements.

(g) Risk of global warming resulting in unusual weather patterns destroying local crops which are supplied to Abexco [coffee]

(h) Change in employment law, including improved minimum benefits to labour, security of employment, increase in the minimum wage

(i) Introduction of trade unions leading to higher employment costs

(j) Introduction of VAT and other taxes resulting in erosion of margins as not all taxes can be passed on by increased sales prices per unit

(k) Sharp fall in demand due to the advent of new technologies. For example, manufacturers of carbon paper, manual telephones, Walkman music systems, Kodak cameras with film rolls, gramophone records, manual and electric typewriters/word processors, audio and music cassettes and players, video cassette recording systems went out of business as technology made their products and manufacturing facilities irrelevant.

It is always better to plan for risk events rather than be taken abruptly by surprise.

Example148: A bank on a Caribbean island has a large number of retail and corporate bank accounts. It has back up information technology servers and systems in the USA which are update every 24 hours. Hurricane Raya hits the island and destroys all physical facilities and systems on the island. Tax havens are not always havens from rainstorms. The bank is prepared for this, has ceased operations 24 hours in advance with notice to customers and has all records at the back up facility in the USA. The backup facility includes parallel processing systems and the bank is soon able to resume operations using the processing site in the USA. Customer confidence in the system increases.

Risks vary over time. The long run risks are different from the short term. Every dictator was elected in the first place because the electorate did not estimate [or heavily discounted] the long run risks.

4.16 Policies and Procedures

Every organization needs to document and implement uniform policies and procedures [PnP] for each function. This is important for continuity and stability of the company, and is therefore equally important for single site, or multiple site companies irrespective of the industry or sector. Once again, as with risk management, it is a mistaken notion to believe that this is a leading practice mainly for banks and financial institutions.

A policies and procedure document for each function will set out the business policy [e.g. employ persons only above the age of 15], the procedural steps to be followed, the requirements for approval and documentation of the process, and the key performance indicators of the process to ensure that the process functions as intended.

These procedures may be documented by way of sequential descriptive steps [narratives] or flow charts together with the relevant section of the authority – responsibility matrix. Procedure manuals work like recipes. They ensure consistency in processing transactions of various types and in addressing different organizational situations. A periodic compliance audit could be carried out to ascertain the extent of compliance with the specified procedures. Policies and procedure manuals facilitate delegation of authority and responsibility. The limits of delegation are clearly defined. They are the backbone of large organizations with decentralized operations.

Example149: A business could have a policy and procedure for recruiting [or not] relatives of current or ex-employees or for doing business with firms of directors. Likewise the business could have a policy about rehiring ex-employees under certain terms and conditions.

Example150: An investment company Ekti could have a policy regarding investment proposals received from a company in which a director of Ekti has an interest or is also a director.

Example151: A contracting company in the business of letting out heavy transport vehicles and earth moving equipment could have a well defined policy on tenders for acquiring such equipment, including qualifications of eligible bidders, procedures for evaluating the tenders etc.

Example152: A company Heidi engaged in producing and selling hospital consumables sets in place policies and procedures for financial reporting including frequency, content, format and applicable accounting standards [local or international]. Heidi also has policies and procedures for appointing distributors for direct and online sales, inventory management, product pricing, recruiting of marketing agents and technical consultants, expenditure on product development [e.g. new types/ sizes and designs of sterile gauzes and forceps], distribution of promotional items and free products, training of users in specialized consumables etc. The finance procedures include procedures for investment of temporary surplus funds, and a dividend payout policy.

Example 153: A company H & R produces, sells and maintains negative vacuum pressure pumps of various capacities and sizes and specialized laser equipment. H & R has a policy of discounts on sales depending upon credit rating and the volume purchased. H & R also has a policy of promotional discounts, quantity based free giveaways, product literature, product training onsite and offsite. In line with the FCPA [foreign corrupt practices act] H & R prohibits certain payments and gifts to customers or their employees. H & R also has a system of budgets and has procedures in the event that budgetary limits are being exceeded.

Example154: An investment company UFIC has detailed procedures and flow charts for filtering of investment opportunities in line with UFIC asset allocation and strategic vision. UFIC also has procedures for assessment of qualifying investment opportunities by the investment head, the risk manager and the investment committee. The head of finance is a member of the investment committee to assess whether the opportunity has the potential to provide a return on assets above the minimum hurdle rate specified by UFIC directors. Before committing to an investment opportunity, the head of investment, in the investment proposal also has to specify an exit route since gains are realized substantially on exit. Exit routes could be trade sale, sale to a private equity fund or even listing on a stock exchange [small cap stocks or an exchange for large cap stocks] or raising additional equity from other existing shareholders and consequential dilution or merger with another company in the same sector by exchange of shares at a agree upon ratio.

Example155: A large chain of hypermarkets Picky Point has over 50 specialized stores for clothing, shoes, household goods and electronics. Each concept has its own brand. The Picky Point warehouse is centralized and containers are received at a nearby port. Picky Point pays the banks interest at the rate of 8% on working capital advances and short term loans. Picky Point receives goods from many countries such as China, Bangladesh, Brazil and Sri Lanka. Pick Point puts in place detailed policies and procedures for reordering different categories of goods. Procedures for reorder levels [setting and review], reorders with existing suppliers, evaluation of new suppliers, approval of new product designs and pricing, procedures for managing inventory at the warehouse and at each store, since a significant portion of Picky Point working capital is in inventory.

Example156: Kena Real Estate undertakes construction projects and engineering supervision. KRE puts in place policies and procedures for submitting proposals for new projects, including for determining pricing and margins for new projects. Kena also determines the amount of time and expenditure that can be spent on a proposal and the preferred ratio of winning proposals to proposals submitted. Kena has a different set of policies for proposals to governmental bodies and institutions where the approval processes are time consuming, a large number of competitive bids are invited and the payment process is riddled with delays. Kena also puts in place policies and procedures for using other design and engineering supervision firms or financial modelling firms on a project if relevant resources for a project are not available in house. Kena has a section on dos and don'ts for engaging in projects in other countries, developing countries and/ or countries which have sanctions imposed currently or in the past. Kena also commits not to employ child labour on its projects.

Example 157: An oil producing company in the government sector HPOC sets our policies and procedures for engaging maintenance contractors, specialist consultants, oil well servicing contractors, fabrication contractors and for hiring of off shore oil rigs. The policies comply with the governmental requirements on compensation, allowances and employment of nationals of the country and quotas for employment of support and engineering staff from other countries. HPOC also requires all of its contractors to produce a Ministry attested certificate that they themselves comply with relevant ISO standards and with the regulations for employment of nationals. Contractors who are unable to comply and/ or produce the relevant certificate of compliance from the Ministry are not eligible to bid for projects above a specified limit.

Example158: A chemical producing company Hardi Chemicals produces waste gases, waste material and effluents during production. The country has stringent laws relating to disposal and/ or treatment of waste and date expired chemicals [the chemical is ineffective or unstable particular date]. Hardi put in place detailed policies and procedures for treatment of solid, gaseous and liquid waste. Waste matter is then to be disposed using specified methods which do not adversely affect the environment and comply with all regulations and laws. Gases for example, with particle microns above 100 per cubic metre may not be directly emitted without further treatment by specified processes. This helps Hardi to bid for government contracts and also builds community relationships and goodwill.

Example159: A company Big Step producing and sourcing carpets and tea could have policies and procedures that ensure that child labour is not involved, minimum wages are paid as per laws and that community development is supported [in terms of $ contributions toward sanitation, education, electrification and water supply projects], that local ground water resources are not unnecessarily depleted. Big Step as part of their social commitment, also has a policy and procedure of employing a certain percentage of homeless persons, women, handicapped persons, visually impaired persons, military veterans, and retired persons. This procedure will identify suitable criteria for identifying such eligible persons as well as the methods and sources of recruitment to ensure fairness in the procedure.

Companies in the USA are known to have well documented policies and procedures. A yellow Dummy's manual for everything. And then, they have non compliance notes about all the deviations, hearings, and investigations and nothing eventually gets done. The Enrons, Madoffs, Wells Fargoes, sub prime recur unfailingly.

4.17 Business Plans

"I used to provide capital for business startups. Here's my card. I'm an angel investor."

Business plans [BP] usually take the form of annual business plans.

The starting point of most business plans is the budgeted sales. The rest of the business plans includes the costs of various resources needed for achieving the budgeted sales.

Business plans would include the following key elements:

(a) Vision of the key stakeholders [shareholders in the case of a company or partners in the case of a partnership]

(b) Mission statement [what the organization intends to achieve e.g. specific market share, specific trade reputation, excellence in particular areas, building of human capital]

(c) Business model. A very common error by start ups is to not define clearly their business model and include this in the business plan

(d) Projected sales, costs and net profits. Detailed profit and loss accounts by line item and location are prepared

(e) Statements of strategy, goals and tactics to ensure that the profitability goals in each segment are achieved within the given time frame. This could include milestones so that progress can be measured and monitored over time instead of periodic snapshots

(f) Overview of competition. An analysis of competition, market share and major developments by competitive firms, new strategies by competitors

(g) Macroeconomic overview of the country/ ies in which the business operates e.g. inflation, employment, taxes, political stability, growth of gross domestic product [GDP], per capita income

(h) Market overview including purchasing power, disposable incomes of target segment

(i) Technological developments and risks of technology obsolescence.

The business plan's financials section should include:

(a) Profit and loss account
(b) Balance sheet
(c) Cash flow statement

Too often, organizations prepare business plans consisting only of the projected profit and loss account.

The business plan will specify in detail the resources needed to achieve the targets:

(a) Funding needed for expansion capital expenditure e.g. new operating locations

(b) Funding needed for increases in working capital e.g. increase in inventory holding and increase in level of receivables in order to support higher level of sales or new product launch

(c) Funding needed for additional purchases of regular capital expenditure e.g. additional warehouse storage equipment such as racks and fork lifts

(d) Additional human resources needed in various departments at various managerial and non managerial levels

(e) Investments needed in real estate

(f) Investments needed in new information technology assets e.g. an ERP system may be needed

A consultant engaged to prepare a business plan will need to have several discussion meetings with the management, review actuals for the year versus the previous business plan and identify the significant changes [nonlinear] in required sales trend, and committed resources.

The consultant will have to carefully identify the critical success factors which are key enablers or which could put at risk the business plan.

Example160: Rash Chemicals has a profitable production unit within the city limits. This unit contributes over 50% of the Rash's overall profits. There is a move by the government to require such chemical units to move out of the city limits on account of environmental considerations.

Example161: Vusco Steel has been set up in a backward district. The plant has been set up to use coal fired furnaces and also has a tax holiday. The government is keen on discontinuing through regulation the use of coal fired furnaces and may terminate the tax holiday.

Example162. Rayon Synthetics has been set up to manufacture polyester filament yarn. The plant is currently profitable and operates at 75% capacity. The management intends to increase capacity utilization. However, a mega corporation is setting up another project for the same product with a capacity which is ten times that of Rayon. Relco will be able to price the same product at around 20% lower than Rayon. Rayon's future is at risk [eventually Rayon sold out to Relco].

Example163: Wypro tech has set up a subsidiary in Silicon Valley and has a head office in India. Wyprotech's basic model is to supply Indian software engineers to large tech companies in the USA. A change in government and governmental regulations makes it difficult to continue to get visas for lower cost Indian software engineers. Wyprotech has to change its business model to carrying out projects offsite in India.

Example164: A national aerated water and cola company Kempa Spot intends to increase its sales. However, a large multinational has recently secured a licence to operate m the country. The multinational starts acquiring Kempa Spot's distributors. Kempa's business plan is at risk of failing.

Example 165: A multinational company Isico sells a range of sweetened energy drinks and sodas in the Middle East. A huge market for them, in addition to their sales to two countries in the EU and within India. Both the EU and the Middle East levy a 50% tax on such drinks as they are deemed unhealthy, high in sugar, addictive and lead to obesity. There is a huge drop in sales.

Example166: Getgo is a low cost carrier in the country. Getgo is borderline profitable and has routes that are not particularly attractive to air travellers. A large south east Asian operator [Airscea] secures a licence. Airscea has the financial backing to offer lower fares, superior aircraft and better services on the same routes, in addition, to connecting flights to relevant overseas and national destinations. Getgo will struggle to meet its sales targets.

Business plans are often broken down into monthly plans [budgets], cash flow plans which are prepared division wise/ for each strategic business unit.

Generally, the lower a business plan can be broken down, the more its chances of successful implementation. The business plan's financials should as far as practical mirror the company's cash generation units [CGUs].

Strategy is the high level underlying direction of the business plan. Strategic direction could involve geographical diversification or focusing only on the premium or lower price segment.

Example167: An automobile company's strategy could be to mass produce lower priced cars or to make premium vehicles or fuel efficient vehicles which command a premium or to make vehicles which last longer thus commanding a better sale price as pre-owned vehicles on resale. The company could also decide to make vehicles which require heavy maintenance expenditure after 4 years thus encouraging the user to purchase another vehicle in the 4th year.

Goals are short term objectives incorporated within business plans.

Tactics are means of fulfilling goals.

Example168: A company has a business strategy of purchasing and selling low cost children's toys. A short term goal would be to develop suppliers in low cost countries such as South East Asia, and product designers in other countries. The tactic could be pricing the product low for mass entry into a high volume market to gain market share. Another tactic could be to add unique features or software to the product to command a price premium. A tactic could be to associate the toy or game with a leading motion picture or a leading movie star or sportsperson.

A company can be directionless without a comprehensive business plan. Usually companies have to go through several iterations of business plans before selecting the optimal looking plan. The business plan would go through several rounds of discussions before consensual agreement or a top down direction.

Budgets could be;

    (a) Zero based. A firm may assume that each year is a first year and not assume that costs or sales will take place at a pace based on the previous year. For example, when processes have been significantly reengineered, or the business model has changed, sources of revenue has changed, the incidence of indirect taxes has changed significantly, a project based firm where costs and revenues are usually one-time based on the requirements of the project

(b) Previous year, plus or minus an agreed percentage based on organizational capacity and market conditions. For example, if a competitor has exited the market there could be a jump in sales, if the market conditions indicate steady state growth of say, 3% then that rate of growth over the previous year may be assumed, if there are plans to add capacity or products or services then an appropriate increase would be factored into the sales figure and activity levels

(c) In the case of a project based firm, the sales would be factored based on the work in progress and the expected pipeline of projects e.g. a consulting firm, a legal firm, a construction firm.

(d) Stretched budgets. In the case of stretched budgets, the owners/ shareholders try to push the operations to deliver a higher than normally expected sales performance. For example if the steady state market growth is 3%, the stretch budget may be based on a 5% growth rate.

(e) Zugzwang budgets. The firm is forced by changes in business or market circumstances to make a change.

Example169: A firm Koltex has gas stations across the State. The imposition of fresh taxes results in a severe decline on the profits of gas stations. To sustain the profits, Koltex must add car servicing/car wash or retail outlets to their chain of gas stations.

Example170: A hospital [Lankavati] pharmacy purchases drugs for its patients from the distributors. A change in regulations results in charitable institutions and research institutes getting a 25% discount on the maximum retail price. Lankavati is forced to restructure itself as a health research institute including setting up a research laboratory in order to avail the 25% discount and stay competitive. The alternative being a fall in patient numbers and the closure of the pharmacy except for critical supplies.

Example171: An automobile component manufacturer Fita produces and sells to national automobile manufacturers, radiators and caps. The heavy vehicle manufacturers are shifting to a newer design, low cost and higher in life, radiator from a Chinese manufacturer Gaileys. Fita must either invest in developing the new product for local manufacture or see its sales fall steadily as the new model is taken up. The Indian first generation automobile manufacturers eventually closed down since they did not invest in research and development, and did not introduce new models. Their profits were simply distributed to shareholders. The protected market [regulations against imports] ensured huge profits and acted as a disincentive to invest in product development.

Stretched budgets are rarely achieved in full or even expected to be achieved in full. Actual performance measured versus budgets can be used to determine incentive pay-outs under various reward schemes. The risk of approving stretched budgets is significant.

Example172: Aymax's [washing machines producer] Board puts in a stretched budget to deliver 8% increase in sales and a 15% improvement in net profits. The management signs up to the stretched budget. Six months into the year, Aymax has achieved only the usual 3.5% increase in sales. However, in line with the stretched budget of 8% growth, hiring went up signifcantly, bonus and increments went up, additional capital expenditure and marketing expenditure was incurred. Aymax's net profit for the period instead of improving by 15%, actually dropped by 2%. The market could not support an 8% increase given the extremely competitive situation and price competition. Sales grew only in line with the overall growth in market demand.

Example173: An air conditioner unit manufacturer Voltex produces and sells 173,000 units each year. The management aims to float Voltex on the stock exchange and sets a short term goal of increasing sales to 250,000 units in the following year. Voltex accordingly, sets out an aggressive marketing and advertising budget. Elgeep an international producer starts marketing a high technology, more efficient range at a lower or comparable retail price [depending upon capacity]. Voltex has committed to an aggressive high marketing budget. Sales fall to 154,000 units with further drops predicted. The increased marketing budget hurts the bottom line.

Budgets are often prepared using different scenarios [discussed below].

At the national level, budgets are usually an exercise in revenue targets to meet expenditure, given limits on the deficits. The politics of the matter usually destroys the economic logic. The common man endures his politicians.

4.18 Scenarios

The following usually require scenarios:

- Business valuations
- Forecasts
- Business plans & Budgets
- Resource allocations
- Feasibility studies

Scenarios are developed by using different variable and different values of variables. Variables could be dependent or independent variables. Often variables are interrelated. Some variables such as governmental taxes, inflation in the economy, climatic conditions are independent of actions by the business unit.

Example174: Different estimates of cash flow, growth rates of sales or discount rates will provide different enterprise values. A firm may estimate different rates of growth in sales across a five year period. This may be based on estimates of growth in market demand, additions to capacity, additions to human capital etc. The rate of growth may be constant across the period e.g. 3% or may be linked to estimates of inflation in the economy, or may vary e.g 2% for the first two years, 3% for the third year, and 5% for the fourth and fifth years. Scenarios of cash flows can also be generated based on probabilities attached to each of the range of estimates.

Example175: A scenario of a competitor product coming on stream and its impact on sales. The firm may assume that the competitor product would have superior features or similar features and lower or similar pricing. The firm may assume that the competitor product may be supported by aggressive entry marketing and would garner x% of market share in the initial introductory period, settling down to (x-%) after a while in the market.

Example176: A scenario of a change in government regulation leading to a fall in demand for a product, such as a higher tax on sweet cola drinks or a higher tax on cigarettes. Papcee markets a popular aerated water. The government is in the process of implementing a heavy tax [50%] on the drink, deemed by the Ministry of Health as 'unhealthy'. This would affect sales and Papcee may assume different percentages of impact on sales growth. Similarly, a company Minar sells locally made cigarettes. The government decides in the Union budget to impose a heavy tax on sale of locally manufactured cigarettes [30%]. Minar may estimate that sales may drop by 2%, or 5% or 10% as compared with the previous year, after considering that the gap between imported and locally manufactured cigarettes is now minimal.

Example177: A feasibility study for a therapy clinic or a specialized treatment clinic could develop different business scenarios based on different levels of demand. This would take into account factors such as competition, growth in population, surgeries carried out in the country, availability of insurance for such treatments, whether such treatments are available at government run hospitals in the country, availability and costs of trained therapists, policies of the Ministry of Labour toward recruiting such personnel from overseas etc.

Example178: A mining company may develop scenarios of production, based on production for sale now or holding for inventory with the prospect of selling later at a higher price. The mining company TMA operates copper mines, some open cast and some underground. Each mine has different production capacities and different costs of production. The price of copper on the LME varies. TMA estimates the price of copper on the LME for the next year. TMA carefully monitors the LME prices on an ongoing basis. Depending on various assumptions of LME prices [e.g. are new production basis coming on stream?] and assumptions related to demand [e.g. economic activity in China], TMA would decide how much ore to produce from each of its mines. In fact during some periods it may not be economically feasible to produce any ore from a particular underground mine as the minimum cost of production per ton exceeds the forecast average price of copper on the LME during the period.

Example179: A portfolio manager in listed equities could develop scenarios of selling equities at various prices [and reinvesting the proceeds] or waiting for the index to rise further. The portfolio manager Mr. Moneyshirt would estimate dividend yields and stock prices for different sectors based on financial results, and then again for specific stocks within each sector based on beta estimates for the stock. Money shirt would then develop scenarios of entering or exiting at specified levels of the index and stock prices in order to develop an optimum scenario of returns to his clients and his own management fees based on performance.

Scenarios help management to take better informed decisions, evaluate risks and take calculated risks. A scenario analysis sets out the possibilities of what could result in an optimistic, pessimistic [worst case] and a realistic scenario.

For purposes of management review, scenario results are often classified as:

(a) Best case
(b) Expected case
(c) Worst case
(d) Optimum expectation
(e) Satisficing scenario. Here the management makes a calculated compromise between expectations based on realities of the business world and internal organizational limitations. For example, the market may suggest a growth rate of 6%, however, organizational infrastructure and capabilities may be geared up to deliver or produce only a 4% growth in revenues. There could be limitations of human capital

or assets such as machinery and equipment due to funding or other constraints.

The consultant may also prepare a range of scenarios for the client to choose from.

Example180: A consultant engaged to perform a business valuation may use the DCF method and apply discount rates such as 8%, 10%, 11%, 12%, 14%, 15% etc. to give the client the valuation number at each of these rates, all other assumptions relating to growth etc. remaining constant in each scenario. The consultant may also assume different multiples for working out the terminal value based on estimated industry conditions e.g. 3x, 4x, 6x 8x, 10x etc. of the fifth year's cash flows.

Then there is always the dark horse which was in nobody's scenario. The tsunami out of hell, the unseeded player who won the Grand Slam. Businesses often need to plan for the dark horse as well.

4.19 Critical Path Method

Critical Path Method [CPM] is used on projects to:

(a) Set out the different paths/ sequence of activities required to achieve the project goal. Some activities are undertaken in parallel whereas others are undertaken in logical sequence

(b) Estimate the time required to complete the project

(c) Compress or better align or schedule activities to achieve a shorter time frame for completion

(d) Denote the costs to complete the project using alternative paths [sequence of activities].

CPM can be used for any type of project, whether complex or simple. There can be macro CPMs and mini CPMs within a macro CPM.

Example181: A CPM may be developed to set up a new school or a new hospital from the point of getting the licence and securing the funding to the end goal of having a fully operational facility. Within the macro CPM there would be several mini CPMs covering the various activities. There would be CPMs for procuring equipment, recruiting doctors, nurses, teachers and support staff, for setting up utilities.

CPMs are represented in the form of charts. Nodes represent completed activities. Arrows between nodes represent the sequence and pull between activities. The arrows are also marked with time [days, hours, weeks, months] as applicable required to complete the activities. Each path can also be marked with the costs to complete that path.

The critical path is the shortest or quickest route to achieve the end result along with all associated necessary activities. The critical path may also be the lowest cost route. The lowest cost route is usually, though not always, the least time consuming route. This is below, what a CPM diagram typically looks like:

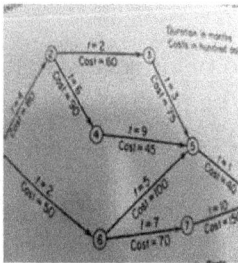

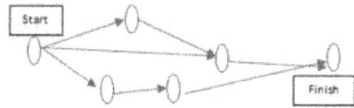

Example182: The CPM for financial model could include steps such as determining the objectives, ascertaining the inputs, feeding in the inputs, assuming relationships between the inputs and the outputs, calculating the outputs, reviewing the results under different scenarios, corroborating the results at least at a high level from independent sources, discussing the financial model with the

client or internal customers. CPM helps in planning the project and also in eliminating or reducing expectation. At each stage of progression, the client or internal customer can be kept informed of the expected time line for completion and delays can be monitored and remedied. The impact of delays on the overall completion time can also be worked out on a real time basis as delays take place.

The CP is not achieved by passing over events or activities which must be completed. The CP for a payment process should not be compressed by eliminating the important steps of checking for original, approved supporting documentation of by not checking for budgetary limits.

The purpose of the CP chart is to understand if more time and resources put into one or more activities can reduce the time and cost to complete.

In addition to project planning, the CP chart can also be combined with the principle of value engineering (4.10 above) to identify activities, processes or project paths which may be focused on with the objective of improving the value-time-cost ratio for the overall project or process.

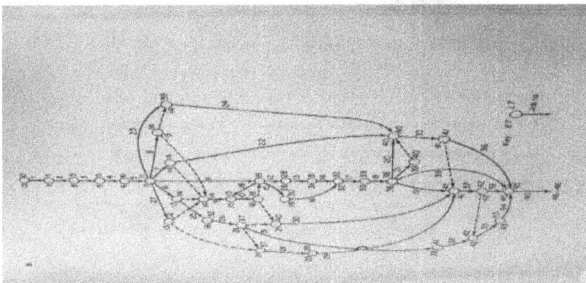

4.20 Feasibility Studies

Feasibility studies [FS] may be undertaken for a number of purposes:

(a) To determine whether a project is financially feasible
(b) To understand the funds required for project
(c) To present to a financial institution or bank or investors for securing a loan

FS are best undertaken by persons with detailed knowledge of the specific sector.

Example183: An industry expert would prepare a feasibility study for developing a solar panel production facility, a waste to energy recycling plant, a gas to liquid energy plant, a school, a hospital etc. The FS often requires technical inputs relating to capacities, technology used, input output ratios and costs of specialized equipment. This information would be essential to building the financial model.

The consultant preparing the FS would need to estimate the prospects of gaining sales and market share. A very good understanding of the costs and behaviour of costs over activity levels is also needed.

Example184: A consultant is engaged to prepare a FS for two young engineering graduates. The project involves procuring used plastic water bottles, reprocessing the bottles and producing 3D printing film for export to EU countries. The consultant would need to know the capital and operating costs of the technology, besides estimating the demand and price of the 3D printing films. An estimate of the quantity and costs of the used plastic water bottles locally is also necessary as procuring them from other locations would be costly [besides transportation].

FS differ from business plans, budgets, cash flow statements and information memorandum.

The consultant also needs to find out from the client who is the intended recipient of the FS. Is it for internal discussion, for bankers/ financial institutions/ private investors. The presentation, format and contents of the FS will differ depending upon the purpose of the FS.

Information memorandum [IM] are prepared in compliance with local regulations with a view to raising funds from a large number of prospective investors. IM usually include forward looking statements [projections] based on numerous assumptions, and favourable statements about the prospects and the management plans/ team. An IM is basically, in nature, a marketing document and not an audit or accountant's report.

A budget, business plan or cash flow statements are detailed, even monthly break downs of financial implications to enable realization of the organizational vision and mission. The budget including cash flow statement helps the founders/ managers to effectively plan their operations given the expected generation of cash by the business, the timing of the cash flows and funding facilities available [such as bank overdraft, short term loans and long term loans or even additional equity available from shareholders.

Not all FS are based on a formally carried out market study. The consultant should make this clear in his proposal to the client, since a market study would entail additional costs.

The FS should state that:

(a) The FS is not an audit or a certification
(b) The FS is based on various assumptions provided by the management
(c) Actual results frequently vary from estimates and depend upon business circumstances
(d) Limit the circulation of the FS to specified users
(e) Specify the methodology of the FS.

Within the FS there will be several snapshots of data in the form of tables, charts, graphs etc. In each case the FS should clearly mention at the bottom the source. The source could be:

(a) Published information
(b) Management assumptions/ budget or forecasts

(c) Consultant's proprietary database

(d) Governmental statistics available with a particular Ministry.

Mentioning the source:

(a) Adds credibility to the FS, and

(b) Enables the client to update the report at a later date.

The consultant should state the period for which s/he is responsible for updating the report. This is because management action or approvals often take a long time and updates cost both time and money, if the sources have been paid for [e.g. publications purchased or database subscriptions].

Remember that feasibility options rarely take into account negative scenarios. The DNA of management is to think positive. Nobody ever sets up a nuclear plant thinking of Chernobyl or Fukushima.

4.21 Intangibles

Intangible assets are assets which do not have a physical form.

Example184: Copyright, product or process patent, brand name, trade mark logo, product formula [perfumes, colas etc.], aviation routes and landing rights, goodwill, franchise fees, licences.

The value attached to an intangible asset is on account of:

(a) The revenue generating capacity of the asset, and
(b) The difficulty of entering or replicating. E.g. difficulty in getting a licence

Example185: A finance and investment company Minfic acquires a brokerage firm Elfic. Elfic has a licence to undertake brokerage activities. Such licences are limited to a few firms and the government currently, does not have a policy for issuing further licences. Minfic can recognize goodwill on the purchase. If the purchase price for

Minfic is less than the estimated value of Elfic, then Minfic can recognize negative goodwill and credit it to the income statement in the year of acquisition.

Example186: Delea has the exclusive rights to market Noks sports goods in a particular country. Delea can recognize an intangible asset. However, if Noks has limited the exclusivity for a ten year period, then the asset must be written off by Delea over the ten year period. The intangible asset will be written down proportionately over ten years according to the use.

Example187. Novat has acquired a lease for a premium and recognizes an intangible asset. The intangible asset must be written off in the books of Novat over the lease period.

Example188: Intangible assets with indefinite life [e.g. a brand name or a licence with no limitation as to period] under international accounting standards need to be revalued at the end of each financial year.

Goodwill needs to be revalued at the end of each financial year. If the projections show a lower value then the entire amount of goodwill needs to be written off. Goodwill is the one intangible asset which cannot be partially written off.

If circumstances show that an intangible asset written off previously, has definitely recovered its value on a permanent basis, then it may be written back to the income statement.

Intangibles are measured and valued according to the stream of benefits that may be reasonably expected to accrue from the use of the intangible. The value of a business would differ if the business were managed without a brand name and the premium which the brand name would attract. The assumption is that the brand either commands a price premium or generates more sales, than would be possible without the use of the brand.

Businesses which are strongly dependent on the value of intangibles may try to introduce the value of the intangible asset into their financial statements. This would cause an intangible asset to be presented on the asset side of the balance sheet with a corresponding increase in shareholders' reserves.

Intangibles may be sold or rented for value [trade license agreements], and this would be strong evidence of the value of the intangible asset.

Example189: A restaurant company holding the brand rights for well-known brand may sell the brand rights for a particular territory/ geography. An airline may let out its landing or aviation route rights or code sharing rights to another airline.

Intangibles are usually valued by the excess profits method, that is, the profits earned by use of the specific intangible over what the normal profits without the use of such an intangible asset would be.

Example190: A consulting team operating with a well-established brand name has significantly higher prospects than a consulting firm say, in the name of 'Nobody & Somebody LLP'.

Intangibles with an infinite life are required to be assessed at the end of each financial year, for impairment. An intangible would be considered to be impaired if there are changes in the market, business environment or the intangible itself which indicate a permanent reduction in the revenue earning capacity of the intangible.

Example191: A competitive similar product is introduced at a lower price, or the formula currently used for the product is now in violation of local environment or health regulations, or a change in local regulations makes it easy for several competitors to enter the market. In the case of the brokerage firm, if Elfic's licence is now open to other applicants, then the intangible asset would be impaired on account of a reduction in market share as a result of new entrants.

Example192: A premium paid for a lease cannot be carried forward if the lease itself ends for various reasons or the landlord plans to redevelop and assume back the lease under the terms of the lease, or if the terms of the lease permit the landlord to re tender the lease after a specified number of years. Whereas intangibles can be impaired partially to record a fall in value, there are three basic additional rules:

(a) Amounts written off are charged to the profit and loss account [income statement] and not to reserves

(b) Amounts once written off as reductions may be written back if circumstances change in the future

(c) Goodwill once impaired must be fully written off and cannot be only partially impaired on the financial statements. That is, a firm can either have .goodwill or not. It cannot have a lower amount of goodwill.

It is said (sad?) that Stephen Hawkins did not believe in intangibles. He found it easier to understand religion than be at peace with God.

4.22 Internal Audit

Internal Audit [IA] is the audit by an organization of its own:
    (a) Operations
    (b) Processes
    (c) Systems, and
    (d) Management reporting processes

An IA may be carried out by an in-house IA department or outsourced to a professional firm. The in-house IA may introduce bias and lack independence. The professional firm may deploy latest analytical and automated reporting tools, also investing in continuing education programs for its staff. In some countries internal audit is mandatory, whereas in other countries, it is only recommended as a good practice.

Objectives of internal audit may be principally:

    (a) Assessing compliance with governmental laws & regulations, and organizational policies and procedures

(b) Efficiency audits [e.g. energy usage, wastage of inputs, machine and labour productivity]

(c) Operations [meeting operational standards and key performance indicators, organizational goals]

(d) Accuracy and timeliness of management reporting and financial reporting. A common internal audit observation is that the monthly management accounts based on which management decisions are taken, simply do not add up to the year-end, annual financial statements. The most common reasons for this are short provisions for expenses and common corporate overhead in the monthly management accounts.

Example193: A company Thermix produces several brands of consumer products. Management takes decisions about hiring, additions to capital equipment and marketing programmes on the basis of monthly profit and loss accounts for each range it sells. At the year-end, Thermix reports an audited net profit of $3.4mn, whereas the monthly profit and loss accounts, cumulatively showed a net profit of $5.3mn. Thermix has paid advance taxes, hired more workers, spent on marketing campaigns and added some capital equipment [capacity] on the basis of the monthly management accounts. A consultant or internal auditor is engaged to fully reconcile the year-end audited financial statements with the monthly management accounts.

IA teams which are focused on efficiency audits may use personnel with engineering or other technical backgrounds.

Example194: IA with engineering background may check whether alternate packing materials with the same bursting strength may reduce packing costs, lower wastage of critical input material through better handling and better processing, lower power consumption through more efficient batch change processes and non-idling of machines, using alternate energy sources for some process initiations, change in design of blades to improve the efficiency of a fan.

IA teams also participate in assessments of operational and financial risks. In many countries it is, unfortunately, not mandatory to have an internal audit even for large companies. In many companies, IA is asked to assume to role of risk management. In some companies, IA is asked to report to the chief financial officer or chief operations officer. All of this reduces the impact of IA and has hampered the development of the IA profession.

IA of the integrity of computer systems is undertaken by certified information systems auditors [CISA] as distinguished from qualified, certified internal auditors [CIA]. Most internal auditors have a professional background in accounting although this is not essential. As mentioned earlier a background in engineering could be very useful especially in manufacturing industries. A pharma company may include pharmacists of research professionals in their internal audit team.

A number of retail firms undertake regular, random checks at store level of cash, banking and inventory. Such firms refer to this as internal audit although it really is merely a form of internal operational control.

Internal audit functions well when it reports directly to the Board and is independent of any of the day to day functions.

In some companies, internal auditors are asked to take up concurrent auditing. That is, all transactions/ investments/ purchases/ payments above a specified value should be reviewed by the internal auditor. This is not the optimum use of the internal audit resource. A key attribute of an effective internal audit function is the random nature of its checks without prior intimation, and without disruption of the business or support function.

Internal audit is a good management tool especially in the case of large, multinationals which are geographically diversified. Such companies [commonly US based] rely on segregation of duties, internal financial controls, operational controls, budgets and internal audits to achieve standardization of operations across countries.

Internal audit like Ebola and AIDS is infectious.

4.23 Financial Reports and Audits

Financial Reports and Audits [FRA] contain useful information. FRA can however easily be misinterpreted.

FRA audit reports should be read carefully for qualifications, exceptional matters, and matters requiring special emphasis. Scope limitations are also noteworthy. These taken together or independently could significantly reduce the utility of the financial report.

Example195: Chemtex has finalized its year-end audited financial statements. The auditor's report includes an emphasis of matter para which states that a claim has been filed against Chemtex for $7mn and has not been provided for although legal proceedings are under way. The net profit in the FR for the year is $4mn.

Example196: Sordidco has undertaken some banking transactions with an affiliate company and a related party. The relevant bank statements are not made available to the auditor. The auditor, LSB is unable to form an opinion on the financial statements because of the scope limitation.

Example197: Deepco has an oil rig that has failed. The rig is critical to the profitability of Deepco. Deepco does not provide its auditors LSB any estimate of the cost and time required to have the rig fully functioning once again. LSB qualifies its audit report.

FRA include the financial statements together with the Notes to the financial statements. Often disclosures in the Notes provide valuable information and insights into the financial health of an organization. The Notes include the assumptions, and the accounting policies applied to develop the financial statements. Similarly, many further details on balance sheet and income statement items are provide in the Notes [e.g. shareholders' equity, fixed assets, intangible assets, receivables, expenses].

Similarly, comparison with previous year's figures usually provides valuable trend analysis. When there has been a significant change of the business, say, for example, the disposal of a business unit or a discontinued operation, then the previous years' figures in the financial statements are altered to make them comparable.

Example198: Nocase is a firm selling different types of two wheelers including scooters and motorbikes. Nocase decides to discontinue assembly and selling a recreational, heavy 800cc bike called Roartar. The assembly line for that model is closed. In the audited financial statements LSB would disclose the profit or loss from the discontinued operation separately, and also exclude the results of operations of Roartar from sales and other costs in the current year as well as the previous year. A Note to the FRA would provide details of the profit or loss resulting from the discontinuance of Roartar.

FRA provides the consultant at a minimum [derived from the FRA] with the following key financial information:

(a) Earnings per share
(b) Net asset value
(c) Growth in sales
(d) Trend gross and net margins
(e) Number of days outstanding of receivables
(f) Cash flows during the year [operating, investing and financing]
(g) Additions to fixed assets
(h) Staff expenses and number of employees
(i) Current asset and liquidity ratios
(j) Extent of bank finance & other loans [financial leverage]

Some companies disclose trend data for key items in the income statement and the balance sheet on separate pages after the Chairperson's letter to the shareholders in the annual report.

As mentioned previously, this type of data can be used for purposes of benchmarking with other firms in the industry.

Example199: A company NiceP discloses in the management's report to the shareholders, a reconciliation of the current year's profit with the previous profit, explaining the reasons for the differences, such as increase/ decrease in sales and/ or costs. This reconciliation is not audited and is marked 'unaudited' in the annual report. NiceP could also provide in the FRA the last ten years' earnings per share, closing stock market price, total assets, total shareholders' reserves, net profit and sales. NiceP goes a step further, and provides information related to market size and market share estimates for NiceP and various competitive brands.

Financial reports like today's wedding gowns are often misunderstood, misinterpreted and short on disclosure.

4.24 Analytical Review

Analytical Review [AR] is simply analysis of numbers. These numbers are typically variables that are related or dependent on each other. Not all numbers are derived from FRA, in fact not all numbers are financial numbers. AR is most useful when quantitative data is compared with relevant financial results. AR gives valuable insights into:

(a) Opportunities for improvement
(b) Strengths and weaknesses
(c) Organizational efficiencies or inefficiencies

Example200: The ratio of labour days to total sales.

Example201: The ratio of sales per square metre of retail space. A clothing retailer Splesh could monitor this metric for the category jeans versus sports clothing to identify which category should be given more/ prominent space in each outlet.

Example202: The number of incoming calls dropped by a call centre as a percentage of total calls.

Example203: The amount of explosives used in a mine compared with the over burden removed in tons.

Example204: The ratio of work in progress to the total production. An increase in this ratio could reveal either inaccurate accounting for work in progress or bottlenecks developing in production.

Example205: The amount spent on returnable containers for delivering a product as compared with the product.

Example206: The amounts of salt and cheese used in a potato chip producing plant. If the quantity is more than the standard specification, it could mean a number of issues from misappropriation of inventory to wastage or malfunctioning equipment.

Example207: The percentage of managers or monthly rated personnel to the total number of employees. The percentage of overtime payments to the total wage bill.

Example208: The amount of rejections by customers and returns as a percentage of total deliveries.

Example209: Average time and costs taken to close lawsuits.

Example210: The proportion of online payments to suppliers, payments through bank transfers and payments through cheques/ drafts / certified cheques. The proportion of sales received through credit card or debit card or cash.

Example211: Amount of printer cartridges used versus the amount of paper consumed.

Example212: Number of personnel leaving as compared with the total number of personnel and the number recruited in a given period, and as compared with a relevant benchmark. The benchmark could be another leading company or a country or an industry standard in that specific region.

Example213: Number of versions of print files to total number of completed print files by a publisher. A higher number of versions would mean more time and costs toward editing and completing the print job.

Example214: The amount of wool purchased or yarn purchased by a manufacturer of textiles to the total metres of fabric produced in a period.

Example215: Proportion of patients at a hospital covered by each insurance company and proportion of patients not receiving coverage. The hospital ScreechER may then realize the need to take on board additional insurance companies used by a competitive nearby hospital BreakER, or to waive charges for processing insurance covers.

Comparing unrelated variables and financial results, however, can lead to erroneous conclusions.

Example216: The analysis of machining defects on days of rain and sunshine may lead to an incorrect and irrelevant conclusion that rain [or sunshine] causes more machining defects. There should be a rational cause and effect relationship between the items being compared.

Analytical Reviews often offer powerful insights into health of the business. Trends in such ratios also help to focus cost reduction efforts.

Often Board members track a company's performance in various areas by periodically checking some key metrics.

Example217: A Chairman of a steel plant may simply ask for the daily VAT or GST payments on dispatches and draw conclusions about production quantity and production mix. This information in Steelat was in fact sourced on a daily basis by the Chairman from the gatekeeper who received all invoice copies of dispatches.

Example218: A home furnishings company Sofest, may compare its sales growth trend with the trend in housing growth and population growth in the relevant income segment.

Example219: An automotive company Vitesco, may review trends in free replacement of parts during the grace service period. This may be used to better design offers during the warranty period. Warranties which sound attractive were offered by GBolt on preowned cars of its popular models for replacement of parts which were not expected to break down during the warranty period.

Studies have shown that analytical capabilities of a chess grandmaster are about that good as a kindergarten back bencher.

4.25 Human Resources

A human resource consultant may be called in to perform several projects for a client:

(a) Prepare job descriptions tailored to the specific firm – this enables recruitment of appropriately qualified personnel and management of performance. Job descriptions should state the name, department/ division, role/ duties, responsibilities and authority. It is a good practice to clearly specify the role and at the end of the job description to include key performance indicators [KPIs]

(b) Develop a competency matrix setting out the competencies which should be consistently demonstrated before an individual assumes a specific role or responsibility, and competencies required of all individuals in specific roles. Example a trainee pilot flies for X hours before qualifying as a pilot. Competencies may have varying degree for different grades of jobs e.g. financial analyst/ senior analyst/ management accountant/ chief financial reporting officer

(c) Develop key performance indicators [KPIs] for specific positions – this enables monitoring of performance and evaluation, particularly in the context of year-end bonus payments. KPIs are intended to encourage improvement in operating performance. Several databases of key performance indicators are publicly available as examples:

Example220: Weeks/ days to close monthly and annual financial audited statements, number of customer complaints, lowered employee separations/ turnover, reduction in number of machining defects, reduction in number of rejected production units, reduction in number of damaged goods delivered, reduction in date expired goods, higher production yields from raw input, lower wastage on the shop floor, lower average finance costs, fewer instances of penalties for violations, more training hours delivered, higher number of sales calls converted to actual sales, increase in sales of high margin products from a product range etc.

(d) Grading of jobs. A consultant may be engaged to grade jobs in order of importance or value expected. Similarly critical jobs may be grouped in the same grade. Job grades determine the range of salary and benefits for each grade. For example, only some grades may be entitled to overtime, children's education expenses reimbursement, travel allowances on vacation, business class travel, travel allowances for family, stock options, medical allowances for self and family, number of days annual leave etc.

(e) Design incentive schemes with specific aims e.g. increasing sales of particular products or reducing costs in a particular area such as distribution costs

(f) Assist with recruitment of specific positions including participating in interviews and administering technical & culture fitment tests. An experienced consultant's participation in the selection process would enable selection without bias and proper review of attributes of the candidates

(g) Carrying out salary and benefits review and survey to compare with market levels for comparable competitors [size, age etc.]. Salary surveys are carried out to ensure that a firm's salary structure is competitive enough and designed to attract the best talent relevant to the firm and its stage of development and strategy.

(h) A consultant may be engaged to carry out succession planning for specific roles or for the organization generally. This is equally applicable to family managed firms as well as larger professionally managed firms. This may include role planning, structuring, management coaching etc.

(i) Training in soft & technical skills for personnel at various levels. Personnel may be coached in skills such as team building, communication, presentation, creativity, innovation, negotiation, project planning, finance for non finance executives, budgeting etc.

(j) Engaging with teams to build quality circles, especially relevant in manufacturing companies, to focus on reducing input and processing costs.

Incentives may be designed by a consultant for clients on the basis of the following principal elements:

(a) Short term
(b) Longer term
(c) Cash
(d) Non-cash e.g. shares/ stocks/ options/ shadow stock options schemes
(e) Allowances and benefits e.g. holiday/ vacation pay and benefits, medical and insurance, children's education reimbursements, further studies or professional membership fees
(f) Location specific allowances e.g. specific incentives to work on an oil rig or in a secluded desert or a very cold area or in otherwise harsh or dangerous conditions [hardship allowances]
(g) Sales based
(h) Margin based
(i) Based on cost control
(j) Based on net profits
(k) Based on return on assets or return on equity

Incentives can be used to drive specific behavior. If wrongly designed, incentives can result in increased costs with little or no corresponding benefits.

An incentive scheme designed to sharply increase sales or profitability over the historical trend may have a 'hockey stick' curve with incentive payouts sharply increasing with incremental increases in sales or profitability.

Example221: A city police department put in place an incentive for patrol cars which consumed more patrol [implying more movement and patrolling]. Patrol teams however, found various innovative ways to show more consumption [including idling when stationery] without actually increasing the frequency or coverage of patrols.

Example222: A purely sales based incentive was issued to retail stores. Sales turnover increased rapidly and so did losses. The increased sales was on account of bundled offers with free giveaways with a resulting poor gross margin. The free giveaways and discounts were not deducted whilst reporting net sales, but accounted for as expenses.

Example223: A diversified group MSH Holding operated 8 brands. The incentive scheme for senior management was first based on sales. That did not work. MSH then put in place an incentive scheme for management based on the net profit of brands. Management was aware that certain brands [Max and Max2] were chronically loss making and started charging expenses of other brands to the income statement of Max and Max2, thereby increasing the reporting profits of the other brands. The Board of MSH Holding then put in place an incentive scheme that aggregated the net profits of all of the brands. Management then started charging brand expenses [e.g. marketing campaigns or market research or feasibility work] to the common overhead pool [corporate office overheads] which was outside the brand income statements.

Incentive schemes should not permit management to work against the longer term of the interests.

Example224: KTac had in place three types of incentive schemes for senior management. One related to operational profits, two related to new brand acquisition and three related to disposal of a business unit [based on cash received]. Senior management understood that the incentive related to disposals in a rising market [valuations going up] was a much higher sum than the incentive based on operations. Senior management teamed up to dispose off two profit making brands [which would have been very good for the long term prospects of KTac], and earned the incentive on the cash received on disposal. Two members of the senior management team left KTac soon after the windfall bonus.

Incentives are distinguished from bonus payments. Bonus payments are usually lump sum payments made to reward past performance. Bonus payments are not always assured of recurring and could be simply one time payouts. A share bonus for example. Incentives, while also based on performance, are usually designed to encourage future performance as well. Incentive payouts are

183

therefore, usually graded to allow for higher payments in slabs.

Example225: A company Funtec declares an unusually high net profit of $58 million, whereas its usual net profit are in the range of $20million. This is comprised of a $28million profit on sales of a business unit and $30million of profits from operations. Funtec declares a usual dividend of 25% in line with previous years' and a one-time bonus share dividend of 5% to all shareholders on the record date. Funtec also pays out a 2% bonus [non expected to be recurring] to the management member responsible for the cash profit realized on exit after their auditors LSB certify the amount realized. In addition, to other management & staff Funtec pays out a regular operating profits incentive based on the operating profits of $30million which are 1.5 times the usual net profits.

Example226: AFF has a problem with very high staff turnover in particular grades of qualified technicians. AFF is seen as a good training ground, however, its salary scales for senior level positions are not the highest in the industry. This encourages good technicians, to join other firms, after a period of 2 years with AFF. To reduce this problem, AFF designs an incentive scheme based on length of service. Technicians who stay with AFF for 3 years are paid a one-time bonus of $25,000 and for each additional year of service an incentive of $4,000 is credited to an AFF accrued benefits scheme. At the end of 5 years, the technician can make pre mature withdrawals of up to specified percentages of the annual amounts and interest/ gains earned by AFF on the amounts of annual contribution, and credited to his accrued benefits account with AFF. This incentive is not a bonus. It differs to a future date the cash incentive payment, and incentivizes technicians to stay with AFF on the expectation of the annual accruals being available for withdrawal after a certain period. The pre mature withdrawals are permitted only for specified purposes such as, acquisition of real estate, higher education or childrens' education or marriage or medical expenses or other exceptional circumstances. Amounts not withdrawn are paid out fully to technicians at the end of 10 years' of service with AFF, together with a further one-time bonus of $25,000.

Example227: CGF is a producer of a popular brand of household electricals such as vacuum cleaners, mixers, microwave ovens and cookers. CGF has a problem of retaining senior management. CGF is listed on the stock exchange. There are a number of new entrants and competitors in the industry and senior management often receives offers from other companies. CGF puts in place a shadow stock option scheme. Management is entitled to a certain number of shadow shares based on a performance scale for each grade. For grade 7, achievement of 100% of the target/ budget results in an entitlement of 4,000 shadow shares. For achievement of more than 100% of the budget achieved, grade 7 employees are entitled to 7,000 additional shares, in addition to the performance bonus. And so on, up to grade 10 [the highest management grade in CGF]. These shadow shares are not real equity shares but credited to the scheme account of the management member at the date of the award with the management member having to contribute no grant price, not even the nominal value. The shares are credited annually with the dividend distributed each year on all other shares and also with bonus shares distributed. The market value of the shares is allowed to be withdrawn unconditionally by the management team member, after a period of 5 years from the credit into her/ his scheme account. This market value could be higher or lower than the value of the share at the time of credit to his account, depending upon the performance of CGF and the stock market index.

Alexander the Great was very good at providing financial motivation to his staff. Perhaps the all time best.

Human resources are sometimes referred to by corporations as human capital, especially corporations short on real equity capital.

4.26 Asset Allocation

A consultant may be called upon to review the allocation of assets of a firm, or to devise a formal asset allocation strategy for the firm. This is applicable to both investment type firms/ banks as well as to brick and mortar operating firms.

This would include a review of distribution of asset over:

(a) Industries or sectors
(b) Products or product ranges or brands
(c) Product category
(d) Geographical
(e) Period: short term, medium term or long term commitments
(f) Risk profile: low risk, high risk or medium risk
(g) Rate of return: low, high medium and as compared with the target, also by product. Geography, industry/ sector
(h) Liquidity of the asset
(i) Payback periods

Example228: An investment company Gulf Intersegment House, may prefer to be diversified across industries and geographies or alternatively, may prefer to be focused on particular industry or geography. For example the company may prefer to remain invested in the oil and gas industry or the renewable energy sector.

Example229: A firm may need short term returns of capital or may accept longer payback periods of cash invested. A firm may not invest in the manufacturing of high capacity transformers since the production and sales realization cycle is fairly long. An engineering firm may prefer shorter term contracts to participation in large, infrastructure type contracts e.g. road surfacing versus bridge or road or dam construction.

Example230: A high net worth individual may prefer to accept low risk, low returns on incremental savings. Highloader may prefer to accept a 2% return on a relatively liquid portfolio with a Swiss bank. Freeloader prefers a 15% promised return on a portfolio with an Indonesian bank focused on equity instruments in Asia. Seesaw prefers bonds with a return of 5% giving a medium risk profile, the bonds being purchased at a discount, and intended to be exited at par or at a premium.

Example231: A firm may prefer to invest in old industries [e.g. paint manufacturing] versus investing in high technology and information technology firms. Suntex invests in industries/ sectors such as water pumps, conventional water purification chemicals, water storage tanks, and water conveying pipe lines [metal and other material]. GlobalTec prefers to invest in solar farms, drip irrigation systems, water recycling and desalination plants

Example232: Retail lending to a large number of individuals with a relatively low default rate versus lending large amounts to a few corporates. Madras Finance lends to distributors for their working capital requirements in the vegetable oil trading segment. Madras Finance also lends to individuals against gold ornaments, and to salaried individuals for purchase of two wheelers [scooters and bikes]. Each class of loans represents a different asset class allocation with a different risk level.

It is important for a firm to set out an asset allocation model. Investing in an opportunistic way, without a well-defined plan, often leads to high risk situations in the longer term, which may not be balanced in the portfolio.

Example233: GFarm, an Indian sells farm equipment in India and in the EU. GFarm has a loan in the EU for its assembly line there. GFarm is therefore geographically diversified in terms of its assets. A fall in sales in one market is likely to be offset by a rise in sales in the other market. Because GFarm has sales in Euros, GFarm's loans for its assembly line in the EU is taken out in Euros. This balances out the risk of fluctuation in the value of the Euro relative to their base currency which is Indian rupees. Finmak invests in listed equities.

Finmak invests on behalf of high net worth clients in blue chip equities in developing markets [GCC, India] and also in blue chip equities in developed markets [USA, Japan]. The fall in one set of markets is offset by the rise in another market.

The danger of asset allocation models is that it is often influenced by leadership. China has a 200 year asset allocation policy, whereas the USA has a 4 year asset allocation policy.

4.27 Corporate Governance

Most firms consciously strive to achieve good corporate governance. This is especially important in large firms with a large number of shareholders who are not directly involved in the operations of the company.

Corporate governance structures are designed to ensure that management decisions, consistently, are not made by one or a few individuals and that the management team acts in the general long term interests of all shareholders. The structure consists of various oversight bodies.

A corporate governance structure typically consists of:

(a) A supervisory Board or non-executive Directors on the Board of Directors. Non-executive directors are required to be independent with regard to the board or the company. That is, they should not be holding shares [except the qualification shares] or a paid position in the company [other than that of non-executive Director] or be related to a Director or a management team member

(b) Not all non-executive Directors may be independent and therefore Board regulations usually require a specified number of independent directors. These are usually specialists from the industry or ex audit partners

(c) A Board nominations committee which reviews and approves nominations to the Board of Directors.\

(d) An audit committee which reviews and approves financial statements, appointment of auditors, their reports & fees. This is to ensure that the auditors retain their professional independence

(e) A compensation committee which usually approves stock option plans, pay grades and increases, various incentive schemes [e.g for support and line functions, compensation for senior management such as chief executive officer, chief operations officer, chief financial officer etc.

(f) Regulations as to the maximum number of committees which an individual may be a member of

(g) Regulations as to compensation for committee members

(h) In family managed firms, there is usually a family supervisory board [called as such] setting out the rights, duties and responsibilities of participating family members and key shareholders.

(i) Risk management committee
(j) Investment committee particularly for investment companies and commercial banks

Additional committees may be formed based on the requirements of the company;

Example234: Benchmarking committee, profit improvement plan committee, strategy implementation committee [especially when a new strategy is being implemented], information technology committee [especially when a new IT system is being purchased and implemented to oversee implementation and realization of benefits], new products committee [for example in an automobile company or a mobile phone manufacturing company which is significantly changing designs and market focus], new market/ territory/ geography penetration committee etc.

A corporate governance structure defines a company by its systems and actions to achieve results in a fair, balanced, transparent manner, consistent with shareholder goals.

Transparency is a key attribute of a good corporate governance framework. Companies with a good corporate governance framework disclose more information about their operations and strategy in their annual report. More information is available to shareholders regarding the operations, opportunities, risks, performance trends, expectations from management, industry insights and bottlenecks. The higher the degree of transparency, the more frequent and detailed are the shareholder communications. The more likely is the company to be valued at a higher market price and attract interest from other potential investors.

Corporate governance, however, is required for the general long term well being of the company, to ensure that there are adequate strategic checks and balances in place and that no small set of individuals control the operations and the destiny of the company without having significant capital of their own at risk invested in the company.

At the end of the day, there is however, one small room and one set of people who run the company, and good corporate governance is their Harry Potter's cloak of invisibility.

4.28   Business Models

The business model of a company determines:

(a) How a firm earns its revenue
(b) How a firm incurs its costs, fixed, variable, short term and long term [sunk costs]
(c) How a firm distributes returns to shareholders

The business model of a firm can change/ be changed from time to time.

The business model of a firm is not always apparent to a shareholder or third party from merely the financial statements of the company or the objects clauses of the articles of association.

Example235: A firm may decide ARCO, as its business model to borrow heavily and enter into new markets, or to use only internally generated earnings for expansion or expand only in existing territories and not take on the challenge of new markets.

Example236 : A passenger aviation company may actually earn the bulk of its profits through tie ups with travel agencies, hotels and through sale or lease of older aircraft to other airlines.   Emirates airlines for many years earned a significant portion of its profits through sale and lease of aircraft to other airlines.

Example237: A large restaurant chain company could actually be earning a significant portion of profits through real estate income. For example, it could build and then rent out large retail space, set up anchor stores and then let out the remainder of the retail space to other firms.

Example238: A software development company in India, could earn large revenues through providing personnel for projects [body shopping for overseas firms], without supervision of these resources or responsibility for the project results.

Example239: A mid-sized or small audit firm LSB, could earn significant revenue through placing senior personnel in the slack season as interim chief financial officers or management/ budget accountants with various clients. Financial statement auditors may undertake one off internal audit or consulting engagements in the slack season. Internal audit firms may book most of their profits on one off consulting engagements selectively undertaken each year.

Example240: An online tele medicine firm ISEEU, could actually be earning most of its revenue through product advertisements and sales on its web platform. Whereas the web platform may receive only a nominal fee from online consultations [the bulk of the fee being directly received by the consultants], the web platform may earn its fees as recurring monthly registration fees charged to consultants and one time registration fees charged to patients.

Example241: A cricket league or baseball league or a Turf club [horse racing] or soccer club could be earning significant revenue not through ticket sales but through fees for transfers of players, revenues from refreshments & entertainment, advertising rights revenue, breeding rights [horse racing] and legalized betting on results of events [licences and/ or revenue based fees]. The actual sports event or its results not being material in the context of the revenue model.

Example242: A movie producer Rashnikanth, could be earning most of his cash profits by showing profits on distribution, and helping to declare otherwise non-tax paid income as legal profits. This of course is not legal, but is Devin's business model. A movie star or a professional sportsperson could acquire agricultural land and show his income as proceeds of unverifiable agricultural income [thus paying out lower or even nil income taxes].

Example243: An automobile company could be making most of its profits through the servicing centres by mark ups on spare parts, or through sales of its pre-owned vehicles, as compared with the few hundred/ thousand dollars profit on sale of a new vehicle. The service centre has a key performance indicator of recommending to customers additional replacement of parts every X000 miles.

Example244: A consumer finance company could earn significant revenues through sharing customer profile data for a fee with consumer product companies, B2C web platforms and insurance companies. Of course sharing information without the consent of the clients could lead to legal issues. Some social media networks earn most of their profits [recorded or unrecorded] through sale of profile data of registered users, whereas the official version of the business model is advertising revenue.

Example245: A doctor Patel, working for a general hospital or a teacher Gujarati in a private school could be earning most of his income as referral fees through referring patients or students to their private clinics or other hospitals for surgeries or coaching classes.

Example246: A cola distribution firm/ bottler or a textile synthetic yarn distribution company could earn significant profits through auction of territory distribution rights, sales of bottles, recycling of empties or recycling and/ or of cops [for yarn].

Example247: A printer or copier company or coffee machine company may actually may earn most of its profits through servicing and selling cartridges or refill packs. In fact the machines may be given away virtually free. A diabetic tester a glucometer may be given away free. The profits are in the needles and strips to check blood sugar levels. Camera may sell for a low price and the profits are/ were in the sales of the film rolls. Mobile phone packages may include especially low prices for the instrument. The profits are in the post paid call charges.

Example248: A personal cargo shipping company could earn significant profits through packing and unpacking at site. The company actually earns only a nominal service charge on the shipping/ transportation which is sub contracted to another large transportation company.

The issue within each business model is which services or products are really delivering value and incurring costs.

Example249: A retail bank Azza Bank, which accepts savings accounts from salaried persons earns most of its profits by promoting insurance, asset management products such as funds, remittance fees and retail lending products to its depositors. The savings accounts by themselves do not earn large profits but draw in customers.

Example250: An aviation company known best for its high profile routes may actually be earning most of its profits from air cargo operations on these routes as air cargo operations are more profitable. AirTimbuctoo flies to Paris and Toronto. AirTimbuctoo earns significant profits from transporting heavy cargo at lower rates than competitor airlines, from Paris to Toronto than from passengers travelling from Timbuctoo to Paris or Toronto.

Example251: A legal casino may in fact earn bulk of its profits from entertainment, sales of alcoholic beverages and restaurant revenues. The casino operations themselves may be incurring a loss. A bar or pub may in fact keep beverage prices reasonable and earn higher income from a smoking area or accompanying food snacks which patrons may find necessary or irresistible.

Example252: A mining company may trade in/ sell or lease large amounts of its non-productive land to real estate developers for market based profits earned while developing industrial areas. The mining company may also earn significant revenues from water bodies on its land, from rights to crossings, and from lease of land for housing and township development. The town possibly continuing even after the eventual closure of the mine.

The business model will also determine how costs are incurred and how cash flows within a company.

Example253: Costs could be incurred at a steady run rate or in spurts depending upon progress of a project, costs could be variable to the activity level or fixed in nature for given activity levels. Costs may even be minimum if revenue is earned from recycling or conversion of waste products. A solar energy generation plant would incur heavy initial capital costs and minimal running and maintenance costs, so also a plastic waste to energy plant or a biogas plant. Some element of distribution could be fixed [costs of distribution vehicles or staff] and some elements dependent upon mileage of the distribution vehicles.

Example254: A hospital may earn its significant revenue through in-patients/ day surgeries/ physiotherapy and post-surgery consultations or through consulting physicians and surgeons. An orthopaedic hospital may earn significant revenues through post-surgery consultations, dressings, recuperative treatment, and physiotherapy treatments. Consulting surgeons may pay the hospital a fixed monthly fee for specific hours of consulting rooms and charge the patients directly or may earn a percentage of the amounts billed to patients.

The business model shapes or encourages particular types of organizational behavior.

Example255: If consultants at a hospital are remunerated on the basis of billings to their patients, they may recommend a battery of procedures and tests from their laboratory, additional periodic consultations, periodic x-rays or scans and even in some instances unnecessary surgical procedures.

Example256: A business model which is focused on high sales or revenue growth, make result in increased sales of less profitable products or a retail finance/ credit card/ personal loan company taking on more risky accounts. A business model which is focused almost exclusively on higher net profit may make the general manager use inferior ingredients/ inputs and cut costs in the short run which may damage the long term prospects of the firm. For example a pizza seller may use an inferior quality of cheese or tomato paste and save money but eventually lose customers. A business model for an airline or hotel which is focused on the high end business traveler may provide a relatively poor level of service to the low cost, economy segment. A business model of a low cost airline may provide poor quality of services even if separately paid for. A chocolate manufacturer managed temporarily by its chief accountant and motivated by higher profits may reduce the quantity or quality of its special coatings to reduce material costs.

Example257: A copper mine CMTassie has limited mine operations. However, the rights to do banking or finance or brokerage and other business in the nearby town, including hotels, retail etc. are exclusively tied by local authorities to the operation of the mine. The mine owner earns his profits from the hospitality and retail segments by keeping the mine open and the town running. There are no other options in the area for hotel accommodation except for the hotels run by the mine owner.

Example258: A private railway operator earns significant revenue through advertisements and through letting out retail space at platforms and adjacent to platforms. These retail spaces may be let out to convenience stores and food counters.

Example259: A tourist travel lodge at an offbeat location has low room rents but earns premium margins on food & beverages, use of the ski slope nearby, ski slope coaches and hire charges for ski equipment.

A north korea or Iran would use a nuclear extortion-sanctions business model whereas a Pakistan would use the economic aid business model, and an Israel would use the ghost of middle east oil supply disruption [since 1967].

4.29   Transactions

Transactions involve any of the following:

(a) Acquisitions
(b) Mergers
(c) Disposals
(d) Joint ventures

Acquisitions involve the following processes/ steps:

(a) Preliminary agreements: These are usually encapsulated in the form of a Heads of Term, Offer Letter or Term Sheet. All of these are non-binding depending on the signing of a contract by both parties.
(b) Due diligence: The purchaser usually carries out a due diligence. This is usually a property asset due diligence, a corporate entity due diligence, a financial due diligence, a tax due diligence, and a labour due diligence. The corporate entity due diligence would cover aspects such as legal structure, licences and intellectual property rights. The property due diligence would cover aspects such as terms of the lease, rent and charges. The purpose of the due diligence is for the buyer to establish the

facts and business circumstances, in order to be able to make a final bid offer. At times, several bidders are invited to carry out due diligence simultaneously. For this purpose a virtual data room or a physical data room may be set up with copies of all relevant documents. In some instances when one party wishes to exclude other bidders, the firm may pay the seller an exclusivity deposit which may either be adjusted toward the final purchase price or forfeited if the purchaser withdraws from the transaction before conclusion.

(c) A final bid offer including amount of consideration offered and terms of payment. In some instances an element of the payment may be deferred upon meeting of certain conditions. In some instances an escrow account is set up with the seller's lawyer/ legal firm and the funds are released to the seller as conditions are complied with or due diligence is completed e.g. returns from stockists of date expired product.

(d) Transaction documents such as the share purchase agreement and the transitional services agreement are usually first drafted by the seller's lawyer. The share purchase agreement will refer to all of the disclosures about the business, the terms of payment, closing & completion mechanisms, the warranties and indemnifications provided by the seller and the buyer. The transitional services agreement provides the scope of transitional services and the compensation for the services, the rights, duties and obligations of each of the parties involved. Transition services may be related to ongoing operations or information technology services or lease transfers or transfers of supplier contracts and banking arrangements.

(e) Various other transaction documents are usually signed for registration of the transfer of shares. The transfer of monies and the exchange of signed contract is usually handled simultaneously by legal firms.

Working capital adjustments consist of an estimated working capital included in the share purchase agreement, and a true up within 30 or 45 days from the closing.

Transactions for mergers are a bit more complex. The stakeholders of the two firms will need to decide the structure of the company going forward. Some divisions may be merged, some simply closed and many employees may be declared redundant in the merged entity. The merger would also involve agreement by both parties on the valuation of each entity, so as to work out the shares of each party in the merged entity.

Most mergers are not successful and result in value lost. In fact many transactions are not successful especially in the case of acquisition because too little attention is devoted to the post acquisition work required. After acquiring a business a large amount of work is required to fully integrate the business into the existing organization structure, implement uniform policies and procedures, compensation & benefits scales, quality standards, publicity and public relations releases etc. Very often this is where acquisitions fail and do not deliver all of the benefits promised at the time of acquisition. For example, if not managed properly, post-acquisition the landlords and suppliers may greatly increase their charges, trade unions of the acquired or acquiring entity may demand increases in wages etc.

Example260: In the case of a distribution company which distributed products to a large number of super markets and hyper markets, after acquisition, the customers significantly increased the costs of shelf display space to the new entity, thus damaging the profit margin.

Also, organizational policies, procedures, practices, salary levels, operating and administrative cultures differ widely. Unless these are quickly streamlined and logically unified, these can lead to huge rifts in the merged entity.

Example261: When an audit and consulting firm disbanded and effectively had most of its senior staff and partners joining another large firm, there were huge differences in the way the organizations carried out marketing, put in proposals, priced work done for clients, salary and benefit levels, incurred expenses on training, decided which types of projects to take up or decline, expense and client entertainment policies etc. Eventually, within two years, there was an exodus of one set of staff and partners to various other business entities. The cultural differences were simply too large to overcome.

Effective budgetary control should be established at an early stage after an acquisition with periodic, even bi-monthly financial reviews to ensure integration. Post acquisition there could be transfers between the parties which may need to be completed.

Example262: Key supplier contracts, leases to property, ownership of intellectual property rights, transfer of control over web sites and social media platform, transfer of information technology licences, transfer of key employment contracts and external consulting arrangements are all key issues in the case of acquisition or disposal.

Acquisitions or disposals sometimes involve disposal of a minority stake. Although the due diligence aspects of a minority stake are similar there are a few differences:

(a) Board representation may or may not be allowed

(b) Participation in management may or may not be allowed by the terms

(c) Transactions with firms of the minority stakeholders would need Board approval

(d) The valuation of a minority stake is usually lower since there is no control over the business

(e) Sometimes a minority stake is given to a key supplier or a key customer or a key manager to ensure continuity and commitment in the relationship[

(f) A minority stakeholder may be specifically excluded from certain guarantees or obligations or duties e.g. compliance with governmental regulations, guarantees given to banker or other lending institutions.

The terms of some acquisitions particularly minority stakes, may involve specifying at the very outset, the exit routes or limiting the exit route:

(a) The minority shareholder may be allowed by the terms of the shareholder agreement to sell her/ his shares only to any of the existing shareholders

(b) The minority shareholder may be required to first offer his shares for sale at his preferred price to the existing shareholders, and only continue with the sale to a third party if none of the existing shareholders take up the offer

(c) Minority shareholders in closely held companies may be forbidden from mortgaging of otherwise offering their shares as collateral for personal or business loans without approval of the Board of Directors. In the case of default on the loans, the shares would devolve as collateral to the bank and then disposed by the bank to a third party/ ies

(d) There may be fees imposed by the company for transfer of minority shares

(e) In the event of a proposed share transfer, the minority shareholder may not be allowed to transfer her/ his rights to a Board of Directors position as this is competency based or relationships based as the case may be

(f) The transfer of a minority stake may not be permitted for a specified number of years from the date of acquisition

(g) The sale of the minority stake may impose an obligation to subscribe to further issues of share capital at a premium, either specified up front or dependent on the valuation of the company.

(h) Dilution clauses may apply in the case of employee stock awards/ options and minority stakes which have not been acquired for cash at par value.

Shares may also be issued to the incoming shareholder in a B class of equity shares. B class shareholders may not be entitled to participation in management, and may be entitled to dividends with a ceiling on the maximum amount of dividends that may be paid out to such shareholders. Like other shareholders, B class shareholders would be entitled to the gain on sale of shares, unlike holders of a debt instrument.

Shares may also be issued to minority shareholders coupled with fixed income debt obligations. These shareholders may be required to provide funds with a fixed return for a fixed period. The amount of such funds being proportionate to their shareholding. Such debt instruments, may or may not be convertible into equity at a future point in time.

Example263: An individual Kamlokov, acquires 15% of a company manufacturing writing pens. The shareholders' agreement signed by him, requires him to provide an unsecured deposit of $2mn on which interest will be paid at the rate of 2% per annum. The deposit is not redeemable, except that at the end of 5 years the deposit can be converted into equity at a premium of 30% over par value [or say, book value at the time of conversion] or at a valuation based on 4x the cash earnings of year 5, whichever is higher.

Warranties and indemnities are often provided around legal claims and tax provisions, at the time of an acquisition/ disposal.

Example264: A company Maruppa, sells its entire equity to a competitor. In the share purchase agreement, it warrants that any tax liabilities not provided for and raised within 36 months of the transaction, will be fully indemnified, if above $5,000 per claim by the tax authorities. It also provides an indemnity for any claims by employees and customers to the extent of $5,000 per claim [claims below this would be borne by the acquirer even if relating to prior periods], a ceiling of $100,000 for all such claims, and a limitation period of 18 months for raising any such claim. For example a customer successfully pursuing a legal claim for damages due to a defective product, if the claim is prior to the expiry of the limitation period and the damages caused are assessed at between $5,000 and $100,000, then the seller would be liable to compensate the acquiring shareholders. The same would be the case if within the limitation period, if any, the tax authorities disallow expenses claimed, giving rise to a tax claim above the indemnity threshold.

The transactions of today are petty in comparison to the transactions of yesteryears. Colonial powers, England, Portugal and France traded in countries in Africa, and Asia. The Eiffel Tower has been sold several times to unsuspecting awed investors.

4.30 Negotiations

Negotiations are an integral part of any business or organization. A consultant may be called upon to assist with, advice, participate in or lead negotiations on behalf of an organization. Negotiations prevent legal action in the case of disputes.

Example265: Negotiations with a supplier, a landlord, an employee, a contract with a service provider, the purchase price of an asset, disposals, separation dues, a share purchase agreement, a transitional services agreement. Almost all forms of contracts or agreements involve express or implied negotiations of terms, prices and costs.

Example266: A water supply contractor Samewell to a large hotel HotelInn agrees a monthly fee with the director of operations. HotelInn's internal approval policy requires clearance from the head of commercial Sarkov. The head of commercial points out that the contract with Samewell has an onerous exit clause. The terms of exit [termination by HotelInn] state that Samewell's contract is for a fixed period of 5 years and can be extended by mutual agreement at the end of 5 years. If however, HotelInn decides to terminate the contract before 5 years, then HotelInn would have to pay Samewell for the loss of profits for the balance period of 5 years and would in any event need to provide Samewell with a 6 month notice of termination. Sarkov seeks to renegotiate the exit terms, in response Samewell seeks to renegotiate the base monthly price.

Strategy for negotiations depend in each instance on the circumstances, the parties involved, and the asset or contract involved.

Negotiation is an art and a skill that is best learnt professionally. A negotiator not having been specifically trained is very likely to come off second best, often, not knowing where s/he has lost out. Very often there are hidden costs to every transaction and these must be unearthed and valued.

Example267: In a share purchase agreement, significant value may be lost through less than fair/ optimum negotiation of warranties and indemnity clauses, leading to post acquisition costs. Significant costs may be absorbed due to lower compensation agreed for transition services and effort.

A negotiator should set materiality limits. In practical terms, some items are simply not 'big' or material enough to be negotiated in detail. And sometimes the negotiator would need to add up [aggregate] all such smaller items to check if cumulatively they in fact add up to a significant value of concern.

A negotiator needs to always keep something in reserve, some positive bargaining points in reserve. There are always likely to be end game surprises, by circumstances or by the other party. It is therefore, prudent not to disclose all your cards up front and to keep something in reserve for end stage discussion.

A negotiator will can use the following starting positions:

(a) An extreme position with very high demands
(b) An optimum position closer to what may be reasonably expected as a preferred outcome

(c) A bargaining position with some positive held back for later negotiations

(d) A hard list of negatives to drive value down, some exaggerated though this may damage the credibility of the negotiator

(e) A negotiator for property may state up front that his budget is $ X,XXXX.

Most sellers have slack and are willing to accept a lower price if the buyer is ready and willing to close. Most sellers expect a negotiation and pad their initial quote accordingly. Buyers may use cash down settlement versus deferred payment as a negotiating tool.

Nibbling is not negotiation and is often unethical and illegal. Nibbling involves agreeing a price and then providing a lower quantity or inferior quality or late payment.

A negotiator should typically review a variety of 'what-if' scenarios before deciding her/ his position.

Example268: A negotiation for a property rent should take into account best, optimum and worst case scenarios of retail footfall and sales at that location. The intending tenant would also look at the impact on cash flows of a lower deposit versus a higher rent and a guarantee. The tenant may strengthen the case by offering market survey data on rents.

Negotiating styles:

(a) No small talk, direct to the point
(b) Personal or social talk before negotiating and getting to the point, build trust and credentials
(c) Excited and passionate, aggressively reacts to each proposal
(d) Calm and thoughtful, not reacting immediately to any proposal
(e) Gun point negotiation, fixed, determined, immovable, take it or leave it
(f) Numbers heavy with detailed analysis
(g) Narrative heavy showing a detailed understanding of the situation through past experiences

A tough negotiator will slow down the process, take more time to respond, not respond in kind, and will always, respond positively pushing forward slowly but surely in one direction.

A good negotiator will come away with some freebies, some favourable conditions or rebates and will convince the other party that the final proposal is in their own best interests. In fact, a skilled negotiator will often start from a point which they know is not acceptable with the objective of getting the other party to propose a solution which in fact was the original preferred solution of the negotiator.

Decide at the outset which conditions are simply not negotiable. Some negotiators will put this up front at the outset and will also hold out threats if a deal is not reached.

Example269: A supplier claiming amounts may hold out that at the minimum he should receive payment of 50% of his outstanding within a week or he would send a court notice. A landlord may state that if the rent is not revised upward by at least 25%, then the tenancy would not be renewed on the termination of the lease agreement.

Cultural aspects of the negotiation are also very important.

Example270: A negotiator of a large conglomerate would negotiate differently with an American, Japanese, Chinese, British or Indian contractor. The British contractor may adopt a trader mindset and negotiate every penny on the table. The Indian contractor may rely more reputation and informal assurances rather than the written contract. A Chinese contractor or a Japanese contractor may record all telephone calls and video calls from the outset, for convenient use in later legal proceedings. An American contractor may rely on sending in somebody to enforce the contract or may be willing to write off huge amounts as market entry costs or as costs of eliminating competition.

Example271: Silence or nodding of the head means quite different, and sometimes opposite reactions in different countries. Companies negotiating sometimes start out by sending in the relatively junior team member, holding back the senior for final commitments or decisions. It is good strategy not to commit the senior or expose the senior to any decision up front.

Some common do's and don't's of negotiations are:

(a) Avoid committing advance payments. Advance payments invariably lead to disappointments, although trade practice may make it impossible to avoid

(b) You can often gain a higher price by add-ons. Example and eye clinic selling spectacles will quote for the frames separately from the lenses, a hotel may charge premium rates for use of the gym or pool or mini bar, many restaurants in Italy charge extra for everything on the table such as cutlery, sauces, tablecloth, napkins etc. Add-ons may also be used successfully by a seller in getting more customers. For example, a doctor carrying out a particular procedure may get more patients with the same procedure cost if he provides bi-monthly follow up check-ups at a minimum or nil cost. A supermarket may get additional customers if each additional purchase of $ XXX entitles the customer to reward points which may later be redeemed for value or like products

(c) Indirect add-ons are quite effective. For example a reduction in price if dues are paid within X days or in advance

(d) Back the negotiation by well-established data but do not release that data up front until the other party is in a position of not being able to refute the data by producing their own data set to counter your presentation

(e) Throw in contingency benefits which may amount to little or nothing but provide the buyer with a higher comfort level. For example a used car dealer may provide a 500 mile warranty on specified parts, not really expecting anything to go wrong in

500 miles. However, the customer comes away feeling more confident of the agreement

(f) Always emphasize the value and benefits to the buyer. Forget about win-win. The deal must look good to the buyer from every angle. Most buyers must feel that they have taken advantage of the seller in some way, even if miniscule

(g) It is usually advantageous to specify a minimum order size e.g. a minimum order for one container, hundred boxes or a minimum invoice amount. Even if the customer requests a waiver, the seller usually comes off better in the bargain. Minimum order sizes can also be coupled with bundling of products together, making it necessary for customers to purchase products which they may have otherwise either purchased from elsewhere or purchased at a later date.

Example272: A producer and seller of sports goods AyD Sports, may offer to retailers, a minimum order size of $10,000 and the requirement that the whole range would be purchased. A sale of racquets would include the need to purchase balls or shuttles [tennis or badminton or table tennis] and a sale of cricket bats may include the requirement to purchase a minimum of approved red or white leather balls. A furniture showroom may sell the whole set for kitchens, bedrooms or studies instead of separate components.

Negotiators can push for discounts:

(a) End of season discount
(b) Store closing or even store closing time discount
(c) Large volume discounts
(d) Group discounts or group relationships
(e) Cash or early payment discounts
(f) Loyalty or first time order discounts
(g) Deposits or guarantees lead to lower prices
(h) Allowing the seller to quote your purchase to other customers. For example, consultants will frequently provide examples of other similar organizations for which they have carried out work

Negotiators can use time limitations effectively.

Example273: Limit the time for a due diligence, the time for submission and finalization of transaction documents, the period of transition services, the period of an escrow account, limit the time for an off-season or a seasonal discount.

A negotiator will sometimes deliberately make the pricing so complex that the buyer has little chance of understanding anything other than one main clause.

Example274: A lending agency has a large number of processing charges, charges for early repayment, costs for services and information, costs linked to inflation indices, for which the retail or even corporate customer does not understand the cumulative impact on the effective lending rate. An automobile seller may be quoting only the cost of the basic no options model, knowing that the typical customer will need a jack, fire extinguisher, both side view mirrors and floor mats at the minimum with bumper cameras and protective body and screen films. A readymade garments seller may charge high fees for tailoring [altering] a suit to a customer's specific length or other requirements. A boat rental company may charge high fees for other services such as wi-fi, fishing equipment, meals, on board stewards etc.

In some instances, the parties to a share purchase agreement, or a franchise agreement set out a clause for arbitration proceedings in the event of a dispute. The jurisdiction for such proceedings is mutually agreed.

Negotiations are best carried out before a price offer is made. Negotiations artfully carried out before submission of a price offer or before submission to arbitration proceedings are most effective, instead of negotiations post the event. It is often the case that it is more productive for a negotiator to wait, instead of plunging into negotiations. The other party kicking off the communications, is in itself, conceding the point of need and weakens their position.

Example275: In an acquisition or disposal, the party initiating the discussions has the weaker stance obviously, demonstrating her/ his need for the transaction to complete.

As with the timing of the negotiation, the venue of the negotiation is also important. The negotiation could be held at the offices of either party, or at an independent location or at the offices of either parties' law firms.

Confidentiality through the negotiation process is critical and channels of communication should be clearly defined. At the outset, the negotiators should specify who would be on telephone conference calls and who would be copied on e-mails. Before the start of each telephone call the parties should clearly state whether the call is being recorded or not, and whether the call is without prejudice with both parties retaining all of their rights.

Before making an offer, the negotiator should be clear about the commercial laws of the country. In many countries, an offer followed by acceptance constitutes a binding agreement even if such offer has been made via e mail.

The principal party should understand that the negotiator's interests do not always match the principal's interests e.g. a lawyer, representative of a co-operative. Quite often there develops a conflict of interest and the negotiator could stand to gain where the principal loses.

The Afghan Front is a useful ploy. One party threatens that the other party agrees or else the consequences are dreadful.

Example277: A landlord may insist on a 50% increase in rent and hint that if the tenant does not agree, he will legally remove the tenant at the earliest on one pretext or the other. A developer may offer a land owner compensation and hold out that if the land owner does not accept his 'fair' offer, then he is in a position to acquire it anyway legally through the Courts. A supplier of a critical raw material may hold out that he can supply the entire quantity to a competitor.

A wooden sword in a negotiation is better than no sword, search for it and use it first.

4.31 Decision Making & DSS

Decision making is a critical and all pervasive part of management. Decision making is often a follow through of a negotiation process. Consultants are often called in to either:

(a) Facilitate decision making through inputs
(b) Review the assumptions for the decision
(c) Set up decision making support systems [DMSS]
(d) Review the impact of decisions
(e) Develop scenarios to the situation and quantify the financial impact of various scenarios.
(f) Defining clearly the issue at hand
(g) Overseeing the implementation of decisions and the financial impact

The first step in a decision making situation is to clearly identify the problem. An optimal decision cannot be taken if the problem is not correctly defined.

Example278: If a doctor misdiagnoses a patient, the recommended or administered treatment would be incorrect with possibly disastrous consequences.

Example279: If an organization misunderstands the reason for high employee turnover, the solution implemented would most likely fail to succeed. An inappropriate change in the recruiting agent or the change in compensation and benefits may misfire.

Decision making is often confused with problem solving. Problem solving does not always require a decision, and decision making is not always targeted toward solving a problem. The tools or skills for decision making and problem solving differ substantially.

The consultant should first try and brainstorm internally as well as with the client to put down a list of possible scenarios, alternative solutions and alternative outcomes without filtering any ideas at the initial stage.

The consequences of each alternative path should be carefully studied for both short term and long term impacts. While reviewing alternatives, it should be noted that:

(a) The path of the decision under each alternative may change mid-stream. The simplest example of this is that there could be alternative routes to go from point A to point B. Mid-way on Route1, the individual may be able to switch and turn off to Route 2. A student who has studied a couple of years of a course in sciences may decide after that s/he is better off training to be a management accountant or chief financial officer or banker

(b) Alternative paths and consequences do not occur randomly or with no pattern. For example: There could be alternative probabilities of given streams of cash flow over a period of years. Some scenarios could have a high probability of occurrence and others could have a relatively lower probability of occurring. The assessment of probabilities and likely financial impact affects the decision making process

Example280: Non installation of a high technology flight control system may lead to problems in flight with aircraft with heavy losses of aircraft and life. The airline, may, however, decide that the probability of such an incident taking place is remote, and therefore, there is no requirement to install such a system.

Example281: A policy on overtime versus hiring more workers, or a policy of increasing the fixed salary versus paying out higher incentives during good times, has very different financial outcomes over different time frames and market circumstances.

Each relevant alternative path should be studied for the related costs and benefits both direct and indirect.

Example282: An increase in taxes may result in a lower level of business activity and a higher cost of implementation, resulting in lower net gains. An increase in prices may result in lower demand or higher demand, if customers are equating price with quality. A marketing campaign for one particular product may not increase sales overall in the long run, as customers may simply shift from one product to another within the same range. An imposition of import duties could backfire due to corresponding duties levied on the country's own exports and possibly a black market. Prohibition in most countries has failed in implementation and led to black markets.

The consultant needs to identify upfront the Critical Success Factors [CSF]. CSF are factors that can result in a poor outcome if not managed.

Example283: A food delivery company guarantees refunds if food is not delivered within 30 minutes of ordering. If traffic conditions have not been assessed and 30 minutes is simply not possible within a given radius, then the company may incur huge losses.

Example284: A production unit may be set up on the assumption of power, water and other infrastructure to be supplied by governmental agencies. This may not take place at the pace promised leading to higher operational costs.

Example285: A drip irrigation manufacturing company sets up a facility in an arid zone. Climate changes result in the area receiving more than average rainfall thus eliminating demand.

Example286: A company is set up to produce or sell hands free mobile phone communication kits and/ or two wheeler helmets. The government either does not pass or does not implement or even withdraws the mandatory requirement. The demand for the product collapses within weeks.

Example287: An automobile company Tetrig, sets up facilities in a country to service and sell diesel driven automobiles at a considerable investment. The country passes legislation that limits automobile emissions, or makes it mandatory to sell only petrol or electric vehicles after a specified date or imposes additional taxes on diesel vehicles.

Example289: An audit firm LSB, takes a fresh licence on the assumption that the Companies regulators will soon make it mandatory for companies [clients] to rotate their auditors or tax advisors every 3 or 5 years. The relevant legislation is not passed and companies in the country may continue with their auditors of yesteryear by merely rotating the audit partner.

The key to effectiveness of decisions is Actions. Detailed analysis and decisions are not helpful if timely action is not taken.

Example290: A delayed resolution of a grievance with a landlord or a supplier or an employee could result in unnecessary legal costs and penalties. A delay in accepting a supplier rebate may only lead to having to accept a lower amount later. A delay in accepting a compromise settlement from a debtor may lead to a write off at a later date.

Decision Support Systems [DSS]: Consultants are often engaged in designing and implementing DSS. DSS may provide management with any of all of the following in a timely and easy to understand manner:
   (a) Relevant data
   (b) Relevant information
   (c) Relevant analysis including trends

Example291:

i. Flight control dashboard systems warning pull ups or direction based on flight path

ii. Dashboard type reports on daily bank balances and daily sales

iii. Real time stock market prices on a mobile phone

iv. Real time or daily sales reports of various retail stores on the mobile phone

v. Management accounts on a monthly basis with product or brand wise income statements

vi. Project progress reports including a Gantt chart

vii. A student's test scores

viii. Weather patterns

ix. Real time commodity prices

Before using a DSS which is available e.g. financial or inventor data within and ERP, it is essential to understand the limitations of the DSS and the manner in which it collects, aggregates and reports or analyses data. For example is a news feed really news or is it paid propaganda?

Additionally, a DSS may report data or information with a time lag, and the report may not be up to date.

Example292: An inventory report on the movement of inventory at a chain of retail stores may not throw light on non-moving inventory at the storage centre or may not adjust inventory for sales of the day. Some items may in fact be out of stock.

Example293: A report on sales may not include the trend of competitor sales or data relating to inflation or other economic indicators such as the central bank base lending rate or latest employment and wage statistics. This may therefore, not be useful to management.

Example294: A financial report on production may be based on standard costs which could be quite different from actual costs and a wage impact analysis may be based on outdated consumer price inflation data. An inventory report which is not updated may show items in stock which are not really in stock and have already been sold.

Management accounts effectively designed could be an important part of DSS. Consultants are often called in to design management accounting and reporting systems. Management accounts usually consist of a periodic income statement for each brand/ business group/ division, and comparisons of actuals with KPIs:

(a) Actual results of the period
(b) Cumulative [year to date 'YTD'] results for the financial period
(c) Comparison with budgets for YTD and for the period
(d) Comparison with the previous year YTD
(e) Analysis of key operating parameters such as non moving inventory, labour costs, capital expenditure, marketing costs, production wastage, production targets for end of year, and cash flow.

In a seasonal business trend analysis is important, whereas in some businesses comparison with industry standards or comparison with competitors is important.

DSS can provide management with:

(a) Data
(b) Information
(c) Knowledge, or
(d) Opinions

The degree of reliability of the DSS depends upon which one of the 4 above forms the basis of the DSS. Clearly, the 4 basis above arranged in decreasing order of reliability.

Example295: A trucking delivery firm QuikServce to a rural post, documents the route for the delivery in order to minimize delivery time performance:

(a) Data: HO to Tanvel is 123kms via national highway 3

(b) Information: Ho to Tanvel is 123kms via national highway 3. After 14kms there is a bridge at which the traffic usually is heavy leading to a 45 minute delay

(c) Knowledge: The bridge is also a railway crossing and the site has been a frequent accident site with fatalities due to a manually operated railway crossing. It may save time to avoid the bridge altogether by taking by pass route 25 before the bridge, off highway 3. This by pass adds another 30 minutes to the time required, however, reduces the delay at the bridge and is safer.

(d) Opinion: By pass route 25 passes at night through a town which is a low income, poorly maintained, and has a low level of security, low sanitation systems and water logging at places [all obviously opinions/propaganda]. There could be no adequately stop off place at the town, and no security from violent hold ups taking into consideration the demographics and low security environment. By pass route 25 is not a route which many drivers prefer [again opinion].

Fake news is of course entirely avoidable and undesirable input in a decision making scenario. Today, there are advertisements and Soviet style propaganda. Very little news, much less information and negligible knowledge in the public domain.

4.32 Cash Flows

The analysis of cash flows [CF] is very important for all businesses. In fact for most businesses, unless otherwise proven, CF is the most important life line indicator of the health of the business. CF includes cash, bank balances and cash equivalents such as deposits. Not monitoring CF implies that the business has an unlimited access to low cost funds or no cost funds.

A number of businesses fail due to inadequate cash flow planning. This particularly true of start-ups. A number of start up's plan for capital expenditure, do not correctly plan for cash burn run rates and within a relatively short period run out cash before they start generating serious cash. Cash flow planning involves proper estimation, and monitoring of:

(a) Cash flows required to manage operations [continued and discontinued]. This is primarily working capital such as funds tied up in inventory, receivables, deposits [with suppliers and landlords etc.] and to pay out monthly overhead such as salaries, wages, power and rents. These costs are period costs and are incurred irrespective of the volume of activity. A new business would need cash sufficient to cover these expenses for long periods, usually at least a year, until business volumes and sales pick up sufficiently to generate enough profits to cover these expenses

(b) Cash flows needed to make necessary capital expenditures for equipment, plant and machinery, fixtures, office equipment, transportation equipment etc. These may increase over time as capacity needs to be upgraded

(c) Cash flows related to funding [financing] activities. New loans received, loan repayments, interest on loans, equity contributed by shareholders, proceeds from disposals of businesses or redundant, if any.

(d) Cash flows related to investing activities. Investment of surplus funds [even if temporary] into bonds or fixed income securities or deposits. Acquisitions of new businesses.

The cash flow statement is the third important component of the financial statements [FRA], which are otherwise incomplete. The CF in fact proves that the balance sheet and that the profit and loss accounts have been correctly drawn up in all material aspects.

The CF also forms a very important input during the valuation of a business in the context of an acquisition or a merger. Businesses which are debt free and cash heavy are valued at a higher number because of the relatively lower risk profile.

Example296: Increases in inventory absorbs cash, and could be an indicator of a downward sales trend, or purchase of inappropriate inventory or non-moving inventory items or date expired inventory not written off. This would reduce valuation and not increase valuation for higher inventory levels.

Example297: Increase in receivable balances could be an indicator of tightening of the working capital cycle leading to cash shortages for payments to suppliers. Receivables could increase for a number of reasons such as to sales to related parties not paying within normal credit period, credit sales without proper credit checks on customers, rejections by customers, returns by customers not recorded or even collections made by company representatives outside the system and not recorded in the books.

Example298: An increase in work in progress shows up as absorption of cash. This could be due to increase in production activity or also due to incorrectly recording inputs at higher weights or volumes [and correspondingly paying out excesses to suppliers] or growing production bottleneck or imbalance in capacities or production equipment.

Example299: A number of Indian businesses follow a system of daily cash reconciliations whereby the cash generated by the business is monitored on a daily basis. Production is valued at standards and expenses are related to the production volume [except for fixed costs which are of course known in advance] and accounted for as per budget estimates. The system is known as 'partha' and gives an early warning signal if the business is not generating cash as planned. Surplus cash is usually invested in the trade or in real estate on a regular basis. Some industrialists in Nigeria with large groups, maintain control over operations by periodically reconciling the cash and bank balances with the various components of CF and reported operational results.

Example300: A company planning large capital expenditures will need to review cash flows for cash generated by the business, dividends needed to be paid out, statutory taxes and fees, loan repayments including interest and principal, loan facilities available, possibility of raising additional equity or availing additional loans, possibility of raising finance by speeding up collections of receivables, reduction inventories and/ or by disposing redundant assets.

Example301: Several family managed businesses, where the bank facilities or loan balances are backed by personal guarantees of the founding shareholder, report a daily cash and bank position to the founding shareholder. This statement starts with the bank balances as per the bank, and adjust this for expected deposits and payments. A week's forecast at least is included to ensure that major payment commitments are covered such as rents, taxes, salaries, utility bills. At times lists of key suppliers outstanding invoices are also provided so that in times of cash shortages, payments to suppliers can be prioritized by senior management/ the owner.

As a principle a business should regularly invest surplus cash flows, even if temporary:

(a) Idle surplus funds represent an opportunity cost as the funds represent an asset on which no returns are earned. This reduces the overall return on assets and return on equity.

(b) Operations tend to become complacent if surplus cash flows are held in non or low interest bearing liquid accounts and the tendency is to spend on expansion of assets or marketing programs. Depending upon the cash forecast requirements, temporary cash flow surplus can be invested in short term or medium term deposits.

Example302: Pfisa sells consumer products for cash and regularly generates surplus cash from profitable operations. Pfisa has an accumulated non interest earning cash balance of $35mn. Pfisa's finance director Mesani hires a consultant to plan a cash flow utilization program. Mesani finally presents a plan to the Board for review [implementation with the help of the consultant]. The plan includes placing $4mn in short term bank deposits at 1.85%, $2.5mn in a medium risk portfolio with a potential return of 5% and short liquidity terms, $15mn for buy back of shares as Treasury shares from shareholders [if the Pfisa's share market price increases, then the shares may be later sold by the company at a premium, the buy back also increases the EPS on outstanding shares], $2mn as regular annual dividend in the month of March, and $10mn as a one-time special dividend. The assumption being that the close knit shareholding group can gain a higher return on their personal investments outside as they are willing to assume higher risks than Pfisa as a company.

Cash is King in every business. No cash, no business.

4.33   Employee Stock Options

Employee stock options [ESOP] refers to the practice and principle of rewarding employees with shares in the company.

This is of particular relevance to companies with their securities listed on a stock exchange but can be used even by companies with non listed equity shares.

Another common misconception is that ESOPs should only be rolled out when the stock price is low. The grant price could be much lower than the current market price.

ESOP can also be used by companies which have already seen an increase in the stock price. The grant price to the employee need not be the current market price and may be at a heavy discount to the current market price, thus reducing the employee's cash outflow.

Consultants are often called in to design or alter ESOP schemes. The consultant is required to determine first the objectives of the ESOP:
  (a) Attract high quality management personnel, or
  (b) Retain senior management, or

(c) Reward senior management for past performance, or

(d) Reward generally all or many grades of personnel for performance, or

(e) Reward a founding partner who works in the business

(f) Pay out a retiring partner/ a deceased partner's family

ESOP is usually granted to senior management. ESOP generally is intended to result in a lower cash payout for the employer and higher reward to the employee.

Employees are granted ESOP based on their eligibility, usually in terms of number of years' service with the company, and meeting performance standards or KPIs.

Employees exercise their rights to acquire shares by paying the company a grant price for the shares. This grant price is usually fixed much lower than the prevailing market price, and this is what provides the benefit to the employee. In many countries when an employee exercises the right to ESOP by paying the grant price, the employee is liable to pay an income tax at specified rates.

The shares [options] in the ESOP vest in an employee after a specified number of years [sometimes years after the grant], and the employee may thereafter, either retain the shares or sell them at the market rate and realize a gain.

A company may actually issue ESOP or shares [thereby increasing the outstanding shares of the company] or design a scheme wherein the benefits are calculated periodically with reference to the difference between the grant price and the market price or valuation of the share. The shares may be valued based on a multiple of the earnings per share [EPS]. In this last instance, shares are not given to the employee [thus not diluting the interests of the shareholders] but:

(a) The benefits worked out are either paid out to the employees annually, or

(b) Invested on their behalf into a pension fund payable to them either as

(c) A lump sum on retirement or as an annuity for a specified number of years on retirement or on reaching a certain age.

Such incentive schemes are called shadow stock option schemes/ plans or phantom stock options.

ESOP if actually issued dilutes the existing shareholders, and therefore lowers the EPS and the value of shares. Companies issuing ESOP usually believe that by giving shares to the employees, they are more committed to the company and perform better. However, studies show that in most cases, employees simply sell their shares and realize the gain as soon as they can. ESOP does however reduce the company's cash payout to employees, thereby retaining more cash for shareholders. ESOP may also reduce the short term employee turnover rate.

In the case of joint venture partnerships and start-ups, ESOPS may be an essential form of compensating founding employees for their initial contributions to set up the business or contribute technology or ideas. Shares issued to founding employees are also called 'sweat equity' and may be given at very low grant prices. Although, in reality, it is more a question of 'sweet equity' and, really 'perspiration' is the right word in the English language, not 'sweat'. Horses and the like sweat, people perspire.

ESOPs may not always be of the same class of shares. A company may issue entitlements of B class shares with the same rights to dividends as A class shares, but with no rights to participate in the management of the company.

Similarly, some company schemes entitle employees to relatively low fixed income bearing bonds which may be converted at a future date into equity shares at a small premium.

Example290: Hindra's company scheme provides that the CEO is entitled to 1mn fixed income bonds bearing a coupon of 2% per annum if the company meets specified profit and dividend distribution targets. These bonds are convertible into equity shares after a 3 year holding period [from the date of award] at a premium of 50% over the par value of $1 per share i.e. at $1.50 per share [the market value of the share being $22 per share, this represents a significant gain to the CEO]. The CEO is therefore, also indirectly incentivized to maintain profit and dividend distribution performance for at least the next three years.

Example303: Telexco is a vehicle manufacturing company. Its key management executives are housed in very expensive apartments in a premium area of the city Crumbay. The apartments' values would represent several years' pay for even the senior management, and these values are expected to rise. These executives would prefer to retain the apartment on retirement. If given away without a charge, the company would incur a loss. Telexco's consultant Mani Singh [MS] devices an ESOP scheme for the executives. MS estimates the retirement age, the years to retirement, the value of the apartment on retirement in each case and the year on year increase in Telexco's share price. Each executive is credited annually with shares of the company in a scheme that does not permit withdrawal except on retirement. MS prepares a financial model which shows that the estimated value of the shares earned [versus agreed KPIs] and credited into the scheme for each executive would approximate the market value of his apartment on retirement, enabling him to purchase the apartment from Telexco, at no effective cost to the executive or to Telexco. The Board approves the scheme. MS joins the company, and is one of the first signees to the scheme.

ESOPs bring home to employees the rewards and risks of commitment to the cause. Much like the fortune seeking soldier of yesteryears or today's mercenary.

4.34   LBOs & MBOs

Consultants are often engaged to advice on and in fact implement LBOs and MBOs.

LBOs are leveraged buy outs and MBOs are management buy outs of a majority or hundred percent stake in a business enterprise.

LBOs occur when an intending purchaser of a business is able to convince a lending institution or a bank to finance his acquisition payments to the seller of the business. The lending institution lends the funds required on the security of the shares and assets of the business being acquired.

Example304: An individual wants to buy an apartment from a seller who wishes to exit and realize cash. The buyer has good credit worthiness but does not have all of the cash to make full payment to the seller. The buyer gets a loan from a bank based on the value [and security] of the apartment being acquired, with the bank being convinced of the buyer's inherent capacity to repay the loan as the instalments fall due. The sale agreement would involve the buyer, the seller and the bank with the bank committing to make payment to the seller when transfer of the registration is complete. The buyer usually makes a 20% to 30% down payment from his own resources [buyer's home equity]. The bank's title or mortgage to the apartment is also placed on register.

Example305: Writlin manufactures a variety of writing and drawing instruments [pens, graded pencils, refillable pencils, drawing instruments etc.] for both school, college and professional use by architects and civil engineers. Writlin is valued at $15mn and this valuation is agreed to by both parties. The buyer has not more than $3mn in liquid funds to pay the seller. The balance is arranged through a bank on the security of 100% of the shares of the company and the assets of the company. The seller receives $3mn from the buyer and $12mn from the bank. The bank's right to the shares and assets is duly registered. The bank gives the buyer a 2 year grace period [moratorium] before repayments start falling due each quarter. The buyer puts in efforts to enhance the performance of the business by adding product lines, signing up new distribution channels, reducing redundant assets and labour, improving product quality, more economical purchasing of inputs etc. The improved financial performance enables the buyer to set aside funds to repay the interest and principal to the bank. The business gains a higher sales turnover and the enterprise value net of remaining debt at the end of 3 years is now $25mn. The original buyer sells the business on in another LBO transaction.

MBOs are buy outs by management.

Example306: An owner of a small/ medium sized private airline taxi or a hotel wishes to retire. The senior management secures a loan against:

(a) Their current savings
(b) Their pension fund accumulated balances
(c) Their retirement benefits
(d) Their life annuity insurance policies

The bank will usually see that the business will benefit from a reduction in the salary bill of the company as the key employees would now be owners.

Example307: The pilots of Unita Airlines were able to gain management rights and a significant equity stake by committing to the banks a pay freeze period and security of their retirement benefits, together with a cost reduction plan such as fuel wastage reduction, aircraft optimization and reduction of non-operational or baggage handling & ticket booking staff through automation. The loan from the banks enables the pilots to pick up enough equity shares to assume management of the Unita through control of the Board.

LBOs and MBOs often get derailed and come unstuck if the promised restructuring and performance improvements do not take place quickly enough. If performance improvements do not take place, then the business is simply burdened with the acquisition (LBO or MBO) finance, in addition to the regular business debt for working capital and fixed assets. The capacity of the business to raise additional finance for expansion is also restricted [by an LBO or MBO] as the bank already has a first right to the assets, unless the business is in a high growth segment.

LBOs and MBOs are not necessarily hostile takeovers, although they sometimes are. The first recorded instance of such, was of course when Caesar was stabbed by senate members in Rome.

4.35 Linear Programming [LP]

Linear programming is a technique of finding optimal solutions given assumptions relating to values of variables and constraints. Developments in LP are as old as 1827 and 1939, receiving a thrust during WW2. LP was used to develop solutions to reduce the army's costs while increasing losses of the other side.

LP is used in the context of business situations to find the lowest cost or maximum profit, using a mathematical model. It is therefore, also called mathematical optimization or linear optimization. Based on assumed values of variables and constraints, LP determines the range of feasible solutions and the lowest cost or maximum profit model. LP is often used in manufacturing, agriculture, transportation and telecommunications.

Example308: Empee makes two varieties of calculators X and Y using two machines A and B. Each unit of X requires 50 minutes of machine A and 30 minutes of machine B. Each unit of Y requires 24 minutes of machine A and 33 minutes of machine B. At the start of the week there are 30 units of X and 90 units of Y in inventory. Available processing time during the week is 40 hours on machine and on machine B is 35 hours. The demand for X is 75 units and the demand for product Y is 95 units. Empee's policy is to maximize the sum of the units of X and Y in stock at the end of the week. How much of each product should Empee make in the week?

Solution:

Let x be the number of X units and y be the number of Y units
The constraints are:
$50x + 24y$ is less than or equal to 40 machine A time
$30x + 33y$ is less than or equal to 35 machine B time
x should be greater than or equal to 75 – 30 i.e. 45
y should be greater than or equal to 95 – 90 i.e. 5
The objective function therefore is to maximize:
$(x+30-75) + (y+90-95) = (x+y-50)$. Solving the equations the answer is the 45 units of model X should be produced and 6.25 units of model Y should be produced by Empee in the current week.

Example309: A company B2S manufactures two types of school bags – A and B and the profit per unit is $3 and $5 respectively. Each unit of A takes 12 minutes of assembly time and each unit of B takes 25 minutes of assembly time. The machine used can work for 30 hours a week, after allowing for down time during change overs. How much of each product should the company produce given the objective of maximizing the profit? Further, the company B2S has been offered the opportunity to add a machine. What is the maximum amount which the company should pay per week for the hire of this machine. Solving the equations simultaneously shows that the B2S should produce 81.8 units of A and 32.7 units of B at a profit of $408.9. The increase in the machine hours changes the machine hour constraint, in fact doubles it. The additional profit would therefore, be $408.9 and that is the maximum amount in the short run which B2S should pay as hire for a week.

Example310: A company TRex makes men's suits and trousers. Each suit can be sold at a profit of $30 and each trouser for a profit of $10. The machine can be used for 40 hours a week allowing for down time and takes 6 hours to make a suit and 3 hours to make a trouser. Customer demand in the shop requires that TRex makes at least three times as many trousers as suits. Suits take up to 4 times packaging material as trousers and it is possible for TRex to pack a maximum of 4 suits a week. Solving the equations simultaneously, TRex should produce 10.667 suits and 1.333 suits with a corresponding profit of $ 146.667

The solutions are mathematical solutions [with their limitations of precision] and can also be solved graphically through the intersection of the relevant lines. The mathematical nature of the solutions means that in real life the solution would have to be rounded off to the nearest practicable working solution.

In practice, LP is extremely useful to generate a range of feasible solutions as an aid to decision making. However, it is not always possible to precisely estimate variables and/ or constraints and resources. These also keep changing in a dynamic environment and do not always have a linear relationship.

Example311: LP could be used by a governmental agency to assist farmers. Assume a farmer Mac, has land of L square miles to be planted with either cotton or tobacco or a combination of the two. Mac has F kilograms of fertilizer and P kilograms of pesticide. Every square mile of cotton requires F1 quantity of fertilizer and P1 quantity of pesticide. Every square mile of tobacco requires F2 quantity of fertilizer and P2 quantity of pesticide. S1 is the selling price of cotton per square mile and S2 is the selling price of tobacco per square mile. The area of land to be planted for cotton and tobacco is denoted by x1 and x2, then farmer Mac's profit can be maximized by identifying optimal values for x1 and x2.

Maximize S1x1 + S2x2
Subject to x1 + x2 less than or equal to L (total area)
F1.x1 + F2.x2 less than or equal to F (total Fertilizer)
P1x1+P2x2 less than or equal to P (total Pesticide)
x1 and x2 are both individually greater than or equal to 0 (Mac cannot plant a negative area. In practice Mac may need to plant at least 1 square mile of each plant).

While such LP models are very useful, in practice, input prices may change, productivity for each crop may change for a variety of reasons (climatic conditions, quality of inputs etc.), the selling price may increase or decrease with a change in the quantity of either crop produced. If a higher quantity of cotton is delivered to the market, a lower unit price may be realized. Also, in the example above the products are not interchangeable. That is, the customer, cannot consume cotton instead of tobacco. If however, the crops were interchangeable, say, for example, coffee or tea or tobacco, then the increase in production of one may result in a change in the selling price and demand of the other crop. The increase in production may result in a shortage of the other product or a demand supply gap or a change in customer preferences. As is the case of cows versus lamb or pork or chicken farming and production of eggs versus sale of roosters etc.

Example312: An oil refinery could use LP models to understand which products downstream could be sold to maximize profit. A transportation company faced with many routes and different demand on each route can use LP to determine how many buses/ aircraft/ vessels should be assigned to each route. A railway company could use LP models to price tickets differently for different periods or even times of the day and to decide how many services to assign to different routes. An aviation company or a railway company can also use LP to determine how many seats or berths to offer of each travelling class, at what price given a budgeted or estimated costs of services.

4.36   Quality Circles [QC]

Quality circles are formed between closely related groups of employees to solve work related problems/ challenges.   The group is also responsible for implementation of the solution.

A consultant could be called upon to form and guide quality circles within an organization. Quality circles were first defined and implemented in Japan in the late 1980s. Quality circles are led by trained facilitators. The author of this book is a trained quality circle facilitator.

Quality circles have been successful in Japan and India in the manufacturing sectors.   In the USA quality circles have failed since the focus in the USA is generally on finding out who was responsible for the problem (assigning blame) instead of finding a solution.

Quality circles use several tools to improve productivity and processes:

(a) Cause and effect diagrams also called fish bone diagrams
(b) Process mapping through flow charts with time and cost dimensions superimposed

(c) Frequency charts and histograms – graphical representations of process productivity or defects

(d) Scatter diagrams of incidence of defects

Example313: A company CGLT produces farm tractors. A model 3GX often fails emission tests versus regulatory norms. A QC was formed consisting of the design engineers to study the problem and introduce engine design changes to reduce emissions in line with norms.

Example314: Company Abruj produces bottled water. Random tests show that the label quality does not tolerate well temperatures higher than 30 degrees centigrade or temperatures lower than 5 degrees centigrade. A QC is formed with relevant employees from the purchasing team to procure better quality labels.

Example315: A coffee shop Petite Blanc sells coffee and various snacks. The coffee machine breaks down frequently needed servicing, repairs and even on occasion replacement. A QC is formed with the objective of defining and solving the problem. The cause of the problem is identified as inadequate training, improper use of the machine, poor machine design and quality, specific poor machine parts quality, poor quality of coffee refill spools, and even unnecessary replacements by the vendor of the machine. A scatter diagram is used to plot the various causes, a histogram is also used to plot failures by cause.

Example316: A mobile phone company 4Gio has started experiencing a high incidence of customer returns for replacement of a particular model UGio. A QC is formed. The problem could be related to the hardware, or software. If related to the hardware the problem could be related to the part/s supplied by an outside vendor/s. If there are multiple suppliers of these parts e.g. battery, the problem may be related to the parts supplied by only one particular vendor.

QCs usually consist of only between 3 to 10 persons with a supervisor who is a trained QC facilitator. Meetings are held in a formal organized way, with minutes of meeting recorded and specific agenda circulated before each meeting. QCs can be used to get around the boundaries of the existing organizational hierarchies, in order to solve problems.

Example317: A company Taksins produces radiators and batteries for automobiles. The radiators have experienced numerous customer complaints recently. A QC is formed not with the designer or production supervisor leading the team, but with the line workers responsible for producing the radiators. The design head and the production supervisor may not even be a part of the QC as they would have a defensive interest in projecting the problem and the solution.

Example318: A company BTex produces heat convectors for retail sales. Customers and distributors have complained about paint peeling off and paint bubbles on some batches. A QC is formed with design personnel. The problem could be with the structure and process of the paint shop, the chemical specifications of the paint, the manual processes related to the application and drying, the temperature of the paint shop, the number of paint coatings, the cooling time prescribed etc.

Example319: A company Iinvest for the past two years has filed its annual report late, after the statutory deadline and the annual general meeting consequently has also been delayed. An independent QC is formed with the Marketing head, Personnel head and the internal auditor. The problems could be inadequate skills of the financial accounting team or head, non-availability of the audit team, qualifications by the audit team, late finalization of the report to the shareholders, late preparation of the corporate governance report, non-availability of the audit committee members to review and approve the financial statements, software problems, difficulties in consolidation of financial statements of overseas subsidiaries, foreign currency and language translations of such subsidiaries, overseas subsidiaries maintain books of account according to non IFRS standards using local accounting standards and conventions etc.

QCs as mentioned previously failed in the USA as the focus was on finding out who was responsible, and on ensuring the sanctity of the hierarchy within the organization. Team effort with teams drawn outside the hierarchy and from different disciplines in a co-operative effort was generally alien to the work ethics in the USA. The focus on QC and TQM [discussed below] is a key reason for the dominance of the Japanese automobile majors and other manufacturing [engineering] companies for decades.

4.37   Total Quality Management [TQM]

TQM is an approach that is focused on long term success. TQM involves all aspects of the organization and focuses on customer service primarily. The goal is to improve costs, quality, time required for production or delivery leading to higher customer satisfaction.

TQM started out as a culture with Japanese manufacturing firms and was later adopted by armed forces wings in the USA. TQM is intended to deliver continuous improvements in the quality and costs of products and services delivered to customers.

TQM was later mistakenly replaced by ISO9000 series of standards. The ISO series and methodology merely resulted in documentation of processes in various areas of the organization. The documentation of processes did not necessarily lead to improving processes. In many cases, poor practices were dutifully documented, institutionalized, and communicated in full compliance of ISO standards. The ISO certifications came to mean little or nothing as they did not imply or even promise any improvement of operating performance. All the ISO certifications did was ensure that operating processes were standardized across an organization for various activities.

TQM in Japan was defined by continuous improvements in product and service quality. Visual displays of process targets e.g. rejections per hundred or thousand parts produced were made at each relevant point on the shop floor. Targets were set per day, per shift, per hour. Machine down time was carefully monitored, waste or rejects were constantly reduced until the rates were phenomenally low in comparison with similar operations in the USA. This greatly reduced overall production costs. TQM in Japan involved definition of quality by customer's feedback, and a systematic, continuous approach of analysis and improvement of processes.

Product issues were tracked and constantly improved, even if the improvements came in small increments at first. Data was constantly collected, shared and visually displayed through boards and cards on the production lines. The USA firms later implemented lean manufacturing which completely missed the point. TQM involves aligning every employee in all functions with customer satisfaction. Every employee in her/ his function realizes is that the ultimate responsibility is to delivery customer satisfaction, reduce costs and improve processes. Improved processes leading to reduced time required and reduced wastage provided business firms with numerous benefits.

TQM in Japan was applied to functions such as human resources, marketing, purchasing, distribution, storage, and finance in addition to production processes. Entire organizations were aligned to the company mission and to service goals. Phenomenal standards of product quality and service times were set by Japanese companies through total devotion to customer satisfaction. Market share was gained through superior product quality, superior product design, very quick delivery times and very low rejection rates or product failure rates.

Example320: TQM in marketing meant that marketing expenditure was gradually focused more on customer requirements and perception, giving the customer more product knowledge e.g. washing machines, detergents. The value generated by such marketing expenditure was much more than marketing spend by American majors which tended to use celebrity sportspersons and actors to promote products.

Example321: TQM in human resources led to recruiting the right staff, training appropriately and remunerating correctly. Leading to lower employee turnover and lower costs by way of recruitment, separation compensation and higher labour productivity.

Example322: TQM in purchasing and supply chain including storage and distribution would lead to lower stock outs, lower inventory levels, lower purchase costs, lower insurance and storage costs, shorter lead time in distribution, lower inventory for distributors leading to higher sales volumes eventually, better cash flow planning.

Example323: A chemical firm Hardea, changed the shapes and sizes of product containers with different volumes, in line with customer requirements leading to lower packaging costs, delivery costs and time and increased sales as the product in the new containers could be delivered directly for use to the customer's production line with no requirement for special storage facilities.

Production systems and product parts were designed in fail safe modes. This approach differed substantially from other countries. Russian engineers for example, reduced product failure by including huge engineering redundancies in the design for example in terms of number of ball bearings, or amount of motor winding or backup systems – this increased product cost whilst making products which could operate in extreme conditions. Engineers in the USA were accustomed to factoring in expected or 'reasonable' failure rates – leading to higher overall production costs and lower customer satisfaction, higher product maintenance costs. Needless to say, manufacturing in the USA lost out to Japanese manufacturers, the highest visibility gainers being the Japanese automobile majors. USA automobile manufacturers' solution to getting more power from automobile engines was to throw in more cylinders.

TQM like wi-fi first was adopted by the armed forces in the USA. Wi-fi [a variant invented by Hollywood star Hedy] was first used to guide torpedoes fired by submarines.

4.38   Six Sigma

Consultants are sometimes engaged to implement Six Sigma [6S] projects. 6S represents continuous efforts to attain predictable and long term stable results including low variations in the process outputs.

The firm will define, measure, analyze and control the output of business processes. First adopted by Motorola, 6S was later adopted by large corporations such as General Electric, Honeywell, Accenture, Verizon, IBM, Bank of America, American Express. JP Morgan Chase, GE Capital, Johnson & Johnson, Texas Instruments, Boeing and others. These corporations mysteriously reported billions of dollars in savings as a result of 6S.

6S is focused on stabilizing results of a process leading to reducing both the causes of defects and the number of defects. Through various statistical tools, the causes of defects are studied leading to reduction in defects, reduced process costs and time, reduced wastage and thereby increased cash profits from operations. A 6S process is one in which 99.99966% of all production units are free from defects.

Lean 6S is focused on reducing process waste in terms of material waste, power waste and production waste generally including consumables, rejects and defects.

Common statistical tools used to study process variations and defects are averages, measures of deviation, regression, coefficients, scatter diagrams, Pareto analysis, histograms, cause & effect diagrams, and value stream mapping [costs, value, time across processes].

6S, however, has been criticized on various grounds. For one, it merely gives fancy names and titles to some streams of TQM. Secondly, benefits of 6S are often not long term and the organization easily regresses. Thirdly, 6S is focused on making process output predictable and stable, and not focused on improving processes and/ or innovation. Some industries require much higher standards than 6S. For e.g. the semiconductor industry involves putting millions of circuits on to chips. A 6S standard of 3.4 defects per million is simply not adequate. Customers are in fact entitled to defect free products on every single purchase. 6S allowed American engineers to factor in an acceptable failure [wastage] rate and did not focus on totally eliminating failures. This is in fact a disastrous long term policy.

Example324: Three firms set up outsourcing call centres [contact centres]. The firm GeTex in America employs 6S and sets a standard for not more than 4 dropped calls per million received. The two firms in South Asia including India and Philippines simply do not drop calls as they have fail safe backup systems to pick up first time dial in dropped calls. Clearly the output and service standards of the firms in South Asia are much higher without 6S.

As with the ISO series, 6S often led to temporary gains, documented processes and nothing much else, with the huge minus of documenting an acceptable process failure rate.

Example325: The failure rates of Japanese and Korean manufacturers of mobile phones, washing machines, microwave irons, vacuum cleaners, office machines such as copiers, cameras etc. is only about 30% [less than a third] of the failure rates of American manufacturers employing 6S.

Unlike TQM, 6S is focused on statistical quality control over manufacturing processes, and can often lack alignment with customer requirements, whilst involving only some functions of the organization.

6S often adds large costs by imposing colors of participants [belts] many of whom are full time designated to 6S projects. As compared with QC and TQM, these colorful, full time participants are often not close to the problem, not being part of the line function, and come up with solutions which are either short term or solutions which are largely impractical in terms of sustainable implementation.

Example326: [Poor implementation of 6S in the USA] A famous fast food sandwich chain setting a 6S based standard for cash shortages, short banking of cash sales by restaurant outlets, and void checks [no charge or discounted customer checks]. This was based on averages over the whole of the business in the USA. Total cash losses actually increased since even those restaurants which were not losing cash earlier, now pocketed cash up to the point permitted by organization wide policy. Short or not booked sales increased after 6S based standards provided restaurants with a leeway allowed to not book a certain percentage of cash sales.

Example327: 6S implementation by pharmaceutical companies in both formulations and bulk drugs with either in house operations or contracted production overseas, resulted in disastrous incidences of product failures e.g. in such industries even a single unit failure is not permissible, whereas, 6S allows failures.

6S simply allowed American production supervisors to standardize the incidence of failures in the long term. In the banking industry, 6S did not result in American banks having a lower default rate, in significantly reducing errors, documentary defects, or in improving accuracy and costs of reporting. American firms followed a culture of looking for fancy titles, identifying the person/s responsible and building structures [often inflexible]. Improved profitability and reduced costs was the focus of 6S rather than customer satisfaction which leads to long term sustainable benefits.

Six Sigma is not to be confused with Sikh Karma and does not involve either the use of headgear or generosity. In fact Six Sigma is institutionalized parsimony.

4.39   Knowledge Management

Knowledge management refers to the organizational practice of creating knowledge bases or repositories, at either the organization, department or even the individual position level.

Consultants may be engaged to develop knowledge management systems [KMS] for an organization. KMS helps an organization to:

(a) Collect key knowledge
(b) Retain it within a formal structure
(c) Ensure regular online, updates, and
(d) Procedures and processes for transferring the knowledge.

Retaining knowledge, by itself, is of little utility if the knowledge database is not updated regularly, and transferred or accessible to those who need the knowledge elements.

In some instances, the consultant is engaged to devise systems which will transfer knowledge to those in need, especially in the process of developing a second line.

Organizations may appoint a chief knowledge officer [CKO] to manage the KMS end to end. The

KMS is particularly relevant to retain intellectual capital developed through training and on the job practice for personnel at various levels. Knowledge may be tacit rather than explicit. Individuals may have knowledge of optimal processes, such processes having been developed over time.

Example328: An engineer or a surgeon trained in the UK, now employed in a developing country, may have devised, over time, practices to ensure effectiveness although the same standards of technical equipment and supplies may not be available.

Individuals should be supported by systems which make it easy for them to upload their knowledge into shared knowledge databases.

Individuals in need, could also query knowledge from experts within the organization, and then upload for future use by others.

Individuals learn by collaborating on projects, reviews during or after a project by seniors, or by developing knowledge brokers. Knowledge brokers within an organization take on responsibility for KMS within a particular field.

Example329: A senior purchasing assistant AJ may be a knowledge broker for anybody within the organization needing to travel to China. AJ has been to China on several occasions for meetings with suppliers and can therefore be a useful guide.

Example330: A legal firm retains briefs of successfully completed projects of each type for future reference, along with risk management tips of what could go wrong and which points were hotly negotiated or contested.

Example331: A Middle East company Caltexco hires expatriate managers and workers from various countries such as Philippines, India, UK, USA, Nepal and others. Certain individuals from each country are assigned as knowledge brokers to help new entrants settle into the country in terms of culture, regulations, availability of goods and services, availability of housing & transportation options, doctors and hospitals, personal care and grooming options, , entertainment options, veterinary services etc.

Example332: An engineering firm Jazra has teams of engineers working on various projects within the country. These include site supervision, design architecture for hospitals, school, residential complexes, and governmental offices. Every

Saturday, Jazra engineers have an open house, wherein they discuss the key challenges faced on various projects, and methods being used to overcome these challenges. Jazra engineers effectively, are learning from each other.

Example333: An engineering consulting firm Latic shares across teams its proposals to various clients. The reasons for successful proposals, the reasons for failure and the submissions of competition [where such information is available formally or informally]. This has helped in the past two years to significantly improve the success rate of Latic proposals for different projects.

Example334: A chain of hospitals and clinics for children called Aplo, operates across a country. Its doctors [not just department heads] are encouraged to upload case briefs and particulars of the efficacy of various treatments for various illness, including reasons for success or failure, short term and longer term side effects. This helps doctors at Aplo to refer online cases and take a look at which medicines have proved to be more effective and delivered quicker results.

Example335: A sports good supplier Jullandhar [JD] from India has established a business presence in the EU during the past 5 years. This includes appointing distributors, setting up offices and subsidiaries, taking appropriate tax advice, hiring employees locally etc. However, only a few individuals within JD actually know the processes required to list, secure approvals, distribute products in the EU and set up establishment in the EU. JD is at risk of being set back years, if these individuals leave JD to join other firms in India or in the EU. JD trains other personnel to work with these key individuals and encourages these individuals to develop knowledge bases relating to practices relevant to the countries in which they operate. JD also rotates into the EU senior management in key positions, into roles in their establishments in the EU.

Consultants developing KMS for an organization:

(a) Often times employees are reluctant to share knowledge, in order to retain their perceived indispensability
(b) KMS needs to be independent and free from bias. E.g for Wikipedia there are controls over who can edit and what information can be added.
(c) The structure of the KMS repository must be designed to facilitate sharing and collaboration as needed. E.g. it is of little use to have hard copies stored in a locked

library, accessible only at specified days/ times and only with a series of time consuming approvals

(d) KMS needs to be integrated with the continuity needs, mission and vision statements of the organization.

The interesting aspect of KMS is that a consultant can put in place KMS for any type of organization, profit or non profit, governmental or non governmental, physical or virtual web based. Every organization and system can benefit from KMS.

Example336: Travel and tourist agency, airline, hospital, school etc. A furniture design company may over time develop a KMS of local artisans and design suppliers in different countries such as Morocco, India, Turkey, Korea. An organic food distributor may develop a KMS related to regulations, practices and supply points for organic vegetables in different countries/ continents. A nuts and confectionery distributor and retailer develops a KMS related to sources of nuts and dried fruits in South America, Iran, Egypt, Malaysia with their local products and flavor coatings. An engineering contracting firm which operates in different countries develops a KMS database of reliable legal firms, labour law advisors, market survey firms, real estate firms/ agents for locating sites, financial advisors, and governmental regulation/ licencing advisors in each of those countries. The database states the types of project specialties in each case.

Example337: A sports team/ player [tennis, field hockey, soccer etc.] which competes in tournaments in different countries and against different players develops a KMS. The KMS is based on inputs from past and current players on playing conditions [weather, facilities, lights, crowds, practice facilities] at different venues, the strengths, styles and weaknesses of various players of opposing teams. This enables team players to prepare better for tours and overseas tournaments, and in shorter time frames. Chess players have thousands of reference games available on specially developed software, various sports have video archives of relevant players and games.

Of course proponents of data security strive to shut down knowledge transfer since they view data as a key asset to be manipulated. The fact is that knowledge is to be shared, sadly, this is against human nature as Ed Snowden discovered.

4.40   Business Forecasts

Forecasts are prepared at some stage or the other by every organization.   Consultants are often engaged to prepare or review forecasts. Forecasts are forward looking statements:

(a) used by management for internal review and discussion on future prospects
(b) For presentation to governmental bodies or regulators
(c) For presentation to current or prospective investors
(d) To substantiate the carrying value of certain intangible assets in the books, especially goodwill and other intangibles with indefinite lives.

Forecasts enable management to take various business decisions about:

(a) Introduction of products, services and operations into territories

(b) Continuity of these products, services and operations

(c) Expansion plans over the life cycle e.g. new factories, new distributors, expansion of the product range

(d) Exit plans for these products, services and operations over the life cycle

Principles of forecasting:

(a) Forecasts are rarely accurate

(b) A range of forecast scenarios should be developed with various probabilities attached

(c) All forecasts have critical determinant variables e.g. rainfall for crops

(d) Actual results should be monitored and compared with the forecasts to improve future forecasts

(e) Forecasts should be periodically revised

(f) There is always a trade-off between time to develop a forecast and accuracy of the forecast

(g) There is always the danger of the objective goal influencing the forecast e.g. a sales forecast may be influenced by the knowledge of what sales level is needed to make the business break even or profitable

(h) All forecast models have outliers [extremes] which should not influence the forecast to accommodate such outliers in the model

(i) Forecasts should avoid evangelical bias [coming from above], organizational politics and market place gossip. The forecast should represent unbiased judgment [hence often times a consultant]

(j) Forecasts in the ultimate analysis are judgmental and do not acquire accuracy through use of software. The software only provides historical data. AI does not forecast.

(k) All forecasts have a margin of error. It is a matter of judgment as to what degree of error is acceptable

(l) Averages do not necessarily add value to the quality of the forecast

(m) It is simply not worth the time and effort [expense] developing a forecast for items or units of sales which are not material

(n) Historical trends and sales data are not always useful indicators as consumer preferences are constantly evolving and reacting to market stimulants. Often times current knowledge is more relevant

(o) Forecasts should take into account physical constraints such as production, storage and distribution capacities as constraining factors

Example338: A vehicle distributor Varisse also services vehicles. The new generation MD, Surya, a family member, starts up trading in pre-owned [used traded and traded in vehicles]. To support the sale of pre-owned vehicles, Surya engages a consultant to develop a Blue Book model. The BB is based on data relating to re sale prices [and forecasts adjusted for inflation] of various models of different years of production. Variables such as whether company owned, driver driven, owner driven, service record, accident record, number of owners [evidenced from the registration book], company serviced or privately serviced, city of registration [condition of graded roads] etc. are factored into the model. The model accuracy is tested by running through it known vehicle data to see what re sale price the model predicts.

Example339: A manufacturer and distributor of vehicle tyres, Neopolis produces 43 different types of tires [sizes and models]. Accuracy of sales forecasts is critical. If the sales forecast is too low, there will be shortages of the product. If the sales forecast is incorrectly skewed toward models

288

which in fact do not sell as well as predicted, there will be non-moving inventory. If the sales forecast is too high, there will be working capital tied up in inventory, additional storage requirements, risk of deterioration in the product, need to promote through price reductions. Not only should the overall forecast be accurate, but the forecast should be good for each model. The production plan is derived from the sales forecast. The sales forecast based on past trends may not be useful if a major local transport company has acquired a fleet of 2,000 school buses to be deployed from the new school year. This has happened because of a change in the governmental regulations requiring all local schools to utilize standardized, approved school buses [a certain number of buses per 100 students for each school].

Business forecasts in reality are only slightly better than weather forecasts given the large number of variables. The trick of course is to mumble through the presentation at a fast pace.

About the Author

Savio Sebastian Gomes has a bachelors' degree of commerce and economics. He also qualified as a chartered accountant, a certified internal auditor and a certified public accountant. His projects have spanned many industries, sectors and geographies. He is also the author of Essays in Economics, a series of 74 essays on everyday economics and business, coupled with fictionalized case studies in Tall Shot Stories. Savio has carried out projects in Kenya, Australia, UK, USA, Holland, Armenia, Saudi Arabia and in over 25 cities in India

Savio now works as a financial advisor to a large diversified family owned group. Savio has studied diverse subjects such as quality circles, value engineering and risk management. He is an FIDE rated chess player having played in tournaments in India, Kuwait, UK and the 2015 world senior's chess championships at Aqui Terme, Italy. Savio has worked as a Director with Ernst & Young, Director with KPMG, Partner with Moore Stephens, and Partner with BDO in different countries.